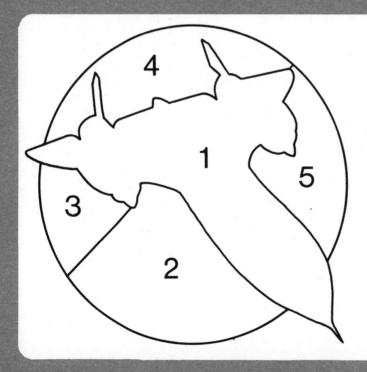

KEY TO COVER

1. The S.R.71A Jet

2. A solar furnace

3. An industrial robot

4. A liquid crystal
   display system

5. The crystal skull

A radio telescope *(spine)*
The mask of Tutankhamun
(back)

Purnell's FIND OUT ABOUT

WONDERS of the WORLD

Purnell's FIND OUT ABOUT

WONDERS
of the WORLD

Artists

Eric Jewell Associates
David Nash
Illustra
Alun Hood
Dan Escott
W. Hardy
John Thompson
Dick Eastland
Angus McBride
Ian Andrews
Peter North
Frank Kennard
Barry Salter
Frank Langford

Written by Neil Ardley

Editorial: Trisha Pike
Liz Graham-Yooll
Graham Marks
Keith Faulkner
Martin Schultz

Produced by Theorem Publishing Ltd.
30/34 York Way, London N1 9AB
for Purnell Books

Published 1976 by Purnell Books,
Berkshire House, Queen St., Maidenhead.

ISBN 361 03500 4

Made and printed in Great Britain by Purnell & Sons Ltd., Paulton (Avon) and
London.

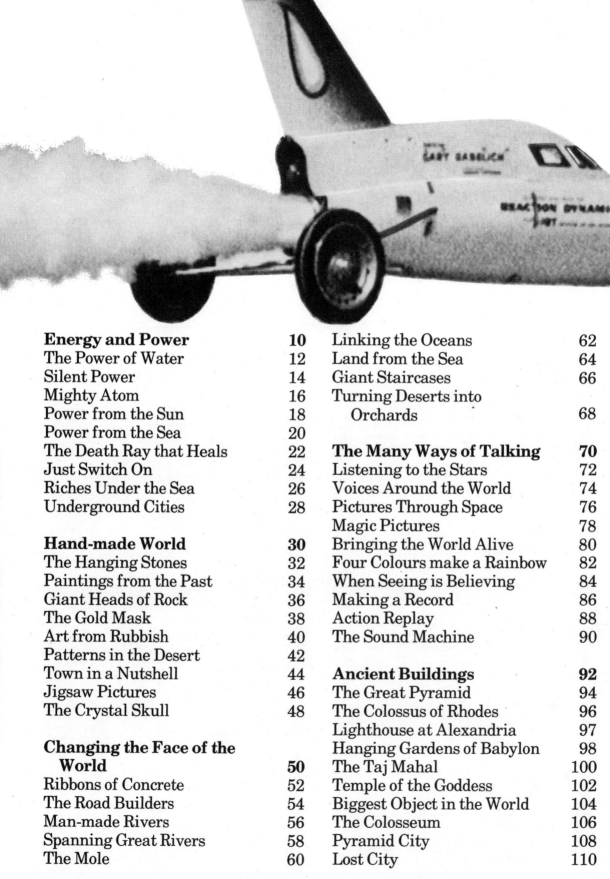

CONTENTS

ENERGY AND POWER

The whole world runs on energy. Power gives us energy. Muscle power gives us the energy to move, and power stations produce electrical energy. Every year man uses up more and more energy. Bigger and better sources of power are needed.

The Aswan High Dam, which is shown below, has doubled the production of electricity in Egypt. New ways of making energy are being found—using the Sun's great power, the power of the tides and the power of the atom—power for the people of the world.

The Power of Water

Falling water has tremendous power. The waters that sweep over Niagara Falls could produce over five million horse power. Hydroelectric power stations use this vast power by changing it into electricity. The stations are placed at great waterfalls, and some of the water is led from the top of the falls down through pipes to a station below. Or they are situated at great dams built across rivers so that a high level of water builds up behind the dam. Pipes from the bottom of the dam lead the water to the power station.

Water enters the station at high speed. The pipes take it to turbines, which are shaped like fans and whirl round as the water strikes their blades. The turbines are

Below: Water stored behind a dam runs through sluices to turn the blades of a turbine connected to an electricity generator.

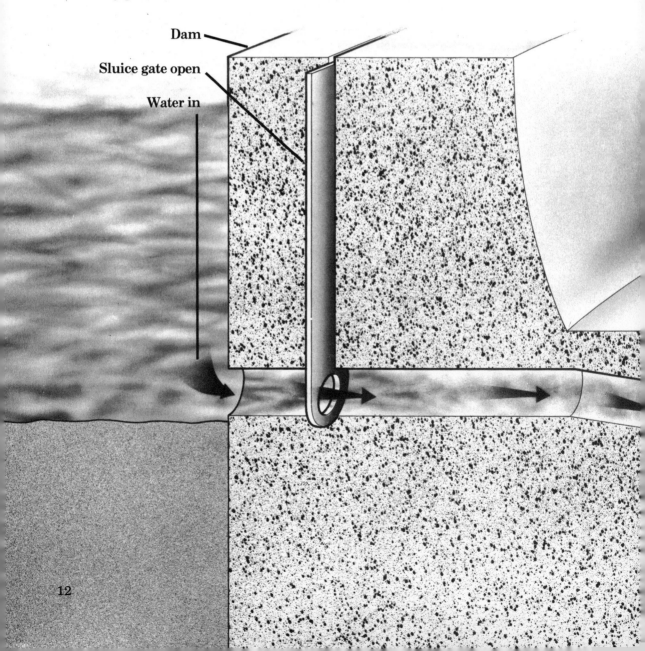

Dam

Sluice gate open

Water in

connected to **electric generators**. As the generators turn, they produce electricity. The water, meanwhile, goes to an outlet and rushes away down river. The electricity is taken away through cables hung from pylons that stretch over the countryside to the cities.

Hydroelectric power is a very good way of making electricity. It produces no **pollution**, and the stations are so clean and comfortable that some are even fitted with carpets! There is no fuel to pay for, and so the energy produced is very cheap, and power production will continue as long as the river is flowing. There are other advantages. The water that builds up behind the dam forms a large artificial lake. In dry lands, water can be taken from the lake and used to irrigate the land and grow more crops to feed and clothe people.

Above: *The turbine hall of a hydroelectric power station.*

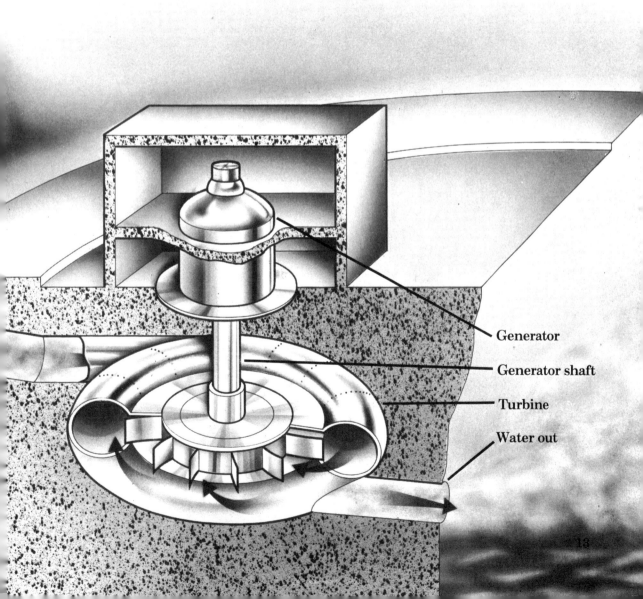

Generator

Generator shaft

Turbine

Water out

13

Silent power

An ordinary power station is a noisy, dirty building. Railway sidings surround the station, and trains clatter in and out, bringing coal or oil to use in the boilers. Smoke from the boilers pours from high chimneys, polluting the **atmosphere**. What a difference from a nuclear power station, which is silent and clean; yet, inside, vast amounts of energy are being released.

Power stations make electricity by producing heat to boil water and using the steam produced to power **electric generators**. Ordinary power stations burn coal, oil or gas in a **furnace**. Nuclear power stations consume nuclear fuel in a reactor. The amount of heat produced is huge. A piece of nuclear fuel the size of a tennis ball produces as much heat as burning 50 railway trucks of coal! To get all this heat, the fuel is simply fed into the reactor; basically, nothing more has to be done.

Nuclear power stations use the metal uranium as fuel. But another metal called plutonium can also be used. Plutonium is made in nuclear reactors from uranium. With special reactors called fast reactors, it is

possible to produce energy and change uranium into plutonium; then the plutonium can later be used to produce energy. These reactors therefore produce a new fuel as they use up the first one!

Nuclear power stations do have some disadvantages. There is no danger that they would blow up like an atomic bomb, but the reactor produces radioactivity—invisible rays that cause severe illness. The reactor has to be covered with heavy shielding to stop the rays getting out. The waste products left over in the reactor when the nuclear fuel is used up are also radioactive. They have to be carefully removed and stored in heavy containers or deep pits. The radioactivity lasts for thousands of years, and so the containers or pits must never leak.

Nuclear power is new. The first nuclear power station opened in Britain in 1956. Now about one-twentieth of the world's electricity comes from nuclear power, but because of the dangers of nuclear energy scientists are now working hard to try to find a safer method of producing energy. Many scientists believe that Fusion Power is the answer; this is the way the Sun produces its heat and light.

Mighty Atom

Man's main way of making heat has not changed ever since he first discovered fire about 400,000 years ago. We use electricity to warm ourselves nowadays, but most electricity is made by burning fuel. However, in 1932 a totally new way of producing heat was found. Man discovered a way of using the enormous energy locked away inside the atom. This energy had been suspected for a long time; in 1895 Antoine Becquerel, a Frenchman, discovered the effects of what we now call radioactivity. His work has been carried on by many people, and our knowledge and understanding of the atom and its power are increasing all the time.

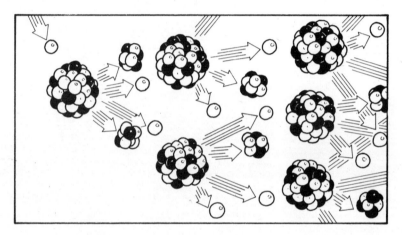

Atoms are very small particles; so small that this page is about two million atoms thick. Everything is made up of different combinations of atoms. When burning occurs, atoms do not change but enter new combinations. When nuclear energy is produced, the atoms themselves change and produce immense amounts of energy as they do so. In fact, very large atoms break up or undergo **fission**. The atoms that do so are those of the rare metals uranium and plutonium. The nucleus (or centre) of each atom breaks apart, which is why this energy is known as nuclear or atomic energy.

Fission occurs in a nuclear reactor. The nuclear fuel is fed into the reactor in the form of rods which contain uranium or plutonium. Inside the reactor, particles called neutrons (which are much smaller than atoms) act like bullets. They strike the uranium or plutonium atoms in the fuel and begin to break them apart. A liquid or gas flows through the reactor and is heated by the fuel. The hot liquid or gas then goes to a boiler to produce steam to power the **electric generators**.

Right: *The interior of the fast reactor at Dounreay, Scotland. The pipes will contain fuel rods, in which the process of nuclear fission produces great heat. Liquid metal takes away the heat from the reactor and it is used to produce steam to drive turbines which make electricity.*

Left: *Nuclear fission starts when a neutron strikes a nucleus of an atom of uranium or plutonium. The nucleus breaks apart, making smaller nuclei and more neutrons. Each of these neutrons may cause other nuclei to break apart, or fission, and give even more neutrons, which cause more fissions and so on. Nuclear fission produces a great amount of heat.*

Power from the Sun

Imagine how hot it would be if there was a small (one-bar) electric fire on every square metre of the ground (about the size of a table top). This is about the amount of heat that is reaching us from the Sun. It is enough to provide us with all the energy we need—if we could capture it and use it.

The giant **solar furnace** in the Pyrenees Mountains in south-west France captures the Sun's heat. Like a

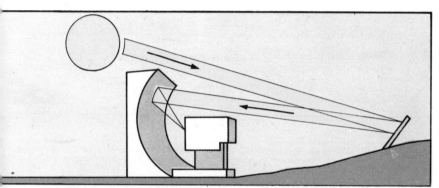

Above: *How the Sun's rays are focused, by mirrors, into the solar furnace. The mirrors behind the furnace move with the Sun so that, no matter what time of day, its rays can be caught.* **Right:** *The furnace built in the Pyrenees.*

giant magnifying glass, the huge mirror of the furnace focuses the Sun's rays at a central point. There, a temperature of nearly 4000°C. is produced. The furnace in the Pyrenees is used as a source of heat for scientific experiments; however, solar furnaces like this one could be used to make cheap bricks and other products normally made in a **kiln**.

Ways of using the Sun's power are being found. You can get very warm sitting indoors near the window on a sunny day in winter, even though it may be snowy outside. Houses and schools are being built that capture the Sun's rays and give warmth. Water can be warmed in large **solar panels** placed on the roof.

Satellites orbiting the Earth get their power from **solar cells**, which change sunlight into electricity. One day, huge satellites in the sky may collect the Sun's energy and change it into beams of microwaves, which are like powerful radio waves. The beams would go to great aerials on the ground, and the aerials would turn the power into electricity. These power satellites may be in orbit by the year 2000.

19

Power from the Sea

What immense power the sea has. Twice a day the level of the water rises and falls by as much as 15 metres as the tides come and go. Could man ever harness this energy and put it to use?

In north-west France a long barrier has been built across the mouth of the River Rance. Pipes in the barrier let the water through as the tide rises and falls. The tidal flow of water turns **turbines** in the pipes, and the turbines drive **electricity generators**.

This tidal power station makes as much power as burning half a million tons of coal every year! Another tidal power station is being built at Passamaquoddy Bay on the border of the United States and Canada. The amount of power in the tides is enormous. By building a barrier eight kilometres long across the mouth of the River Severn in England, up to 10,000 megawatts of power could be generated. This is about equal to the power output of all Britain's nuclear power stations. Such a tidal power station would be very expensive. But, once built, the station would produce cheap power for as long as we need it.

Waves produce great power too. There is enough energy in every metre of an ocean wave to supply a hundred homes with their needs. Getting this energy from the waves will not be easy. But experiments are going ahead to float lines of vanes (metal paddles) in the sea. As the waves rock the vanes, the motion of the vanes will be turned into electricity. Like tidal power and hydroelectric power, we will always have wave power.

Above: *The tidal power station built across the estuary of the River Rance in France. As the tides rise and fall, water flows through turbo-generators in the barrage, producing electricity.*

Left: *Building the barrage of the Rance power station.*

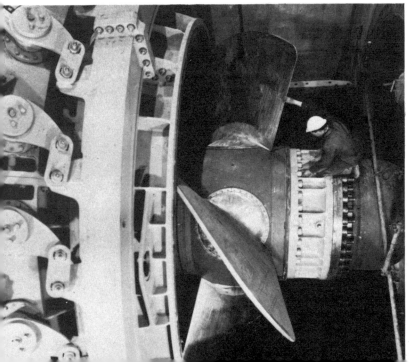

Left: *Installing the turbines in the Rance power station. The turbines are constructed so that they will turn when water flows through them in either direction.*

21

Death Ray that Heals

In 1960 an American scientist discovered a way of producing a beam of light far stronger than any ever produced before—even stronger than the Sun. The initial letters of this machine spelt out a new word—LASER! If a laser beam is focused by a magnifying glass, it burns ferociously.

A laser beam can cut through metal, and it can even drill a hole through a diamond, which is the hardest substance known. **Dies** for making wire are made in this way. A portable laser could be used as a ray gun powerful enough to set clothes on fire, and a large laser could produce a death ray.

However, the laser is much more use to us than just as a weapon. In medicine, lasers can perform delicate eye operations and destroy unwanted growths without cutting open any part of the body. Lasers can also be used to

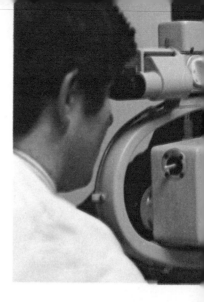

Above: *A surgeon uses a laser to perform a delicate eye operation, curing partial blindness.*

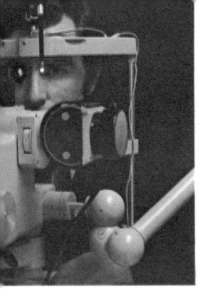

drill out decay from teeth without any pain. Laser beams are needle thin and do not spread out like ordinary light beams. A laser beam fired from the Earth at the Moon is only three kilometres wide when it strikes the Moon after travelling 382,400 kilometres. The beams are aimed at mirrors placed on the Moon by astronauts. By measuring on special instruments the time it takes a laser beam to get to the Moon and back, the exact distance of the Moon can be found.

But the most extraordinary use of lasers is a new science called holography. This is a kind of photography that produces solid images, not flat pictures as in a normal photograph. You can even walk round a holographic image and look at the other side of it! This development may one day give us television or cinema pictures that look completely like real life. This means that an exhibition in a museum in one country can be seen at the same time in many other museums throughout the world.

Below: *A laser beam cuts through a sheet of steel. Lasers are also used to cut cloth.*

Just switch on

Electricity really makes life easy for us. Wherever there is a supply of **current** you can plug in a fire to be warm, connect up a light to read by, or use any kind of electric machine from an electric drill to a vacuum cleaner. Of course, electricity is not absolutely necessary to get warm, have light, make a hole or clean the carpet. But it saves carrying fuel to the house and saves time and effort in looking after a home. Also, electric light is much brighter and easier on the eyes than the dim light of candles or oil lamps.

How does electricity get to the home? Huge amounts of electric current are produced at a power station—usually enough to supply a small city. The power stations in a region are all connected together so that if one fails then no particular area will be without electricity. The

Above: *Huge pylons disappearing over the horizon carry electricity from power stations to homes and factories.*
Right: *An illustration of an electric light cut away to show the inside of the light bulb and how it works.*

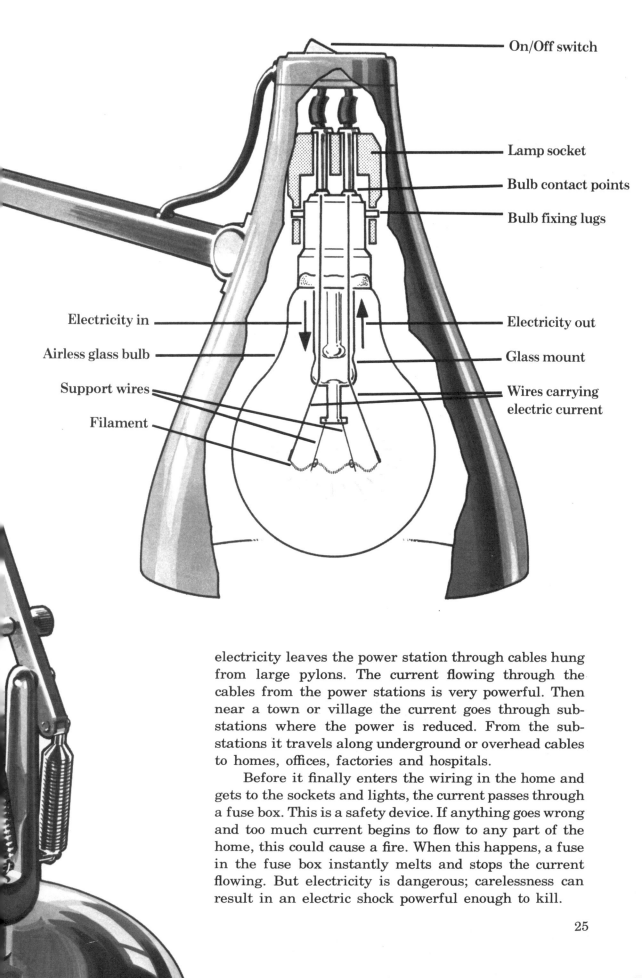

On/Off switch

Lamp socket

Bulb contact points

Bulb fixing lugs

Electricity in

Electricity out

Airless glass bulb

Glass mount

Support wires

Wires carrying
electric current

Filament

electricity leaves the power station through cables hung
from large pylons. The current flowing through the
cables from the power stations is very powerful. Then
near a town or village the current goes through sub-
stations where the power is reduced. From the sub-
stations it travels along underground or overhead cables
to homes, offices, factories and hospitals.

Before it finally enters the wiring in the home and
gets to the sockets and lights, the current passes through
a fuse box. This is a safety device. If anything goes wrong
and too much current begins to flow to any part of the
home, this could cause a fire. When this happens, a fuse
in the fuse box instantly melts and stops the current
flowing. But electricity is dangerous; carelessness can
result in an electric shock powerful enough to kill.

Riches Under the Sea

A strange new 'city' is rising in one of the most unlikely places on Earth—the middle of the North Sea. These were once lonely waters, crossed only by fishing boats or ferries sailing between Britain and Norway, Denmark or Holland. Now, the sea is dotted with gigantic structures, each one larger than the biggest cathedral or office block of any city on the mainland. Helicopters and supply ships bring this new 'city' its men and materials.

The reason for all this activity is the search for power. Beneath the sea bed lie huge quantities of oil and gas, both vital sources of power for industries and homes.

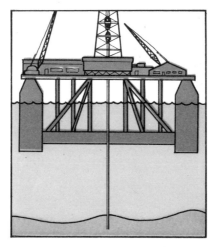

Opposite page: *An aerial view of a North Sea oil rig at work.* **Left:** *Some rigs float on hulls that are half submerged in the water. They are anchored firmly in position, so that they do not move during stormy weather.*

The buildings of this new 'city' are drilling rigs. They either stand on huge legs sunk into the sea bed or they float on great submerged **hulls** and are anchored into position. The sea is often deep—as much as 200 metres—so most of the rig is underwater. But the deck may be as large as a football ground. On it stands a derrick, a tall framework from which a drill extends down to the sea bed, and there are also buildings to house the **crew** and a helicopter landing pad. The oil or gas may lie several kilometres below. When it is reached, it rises through **boreholes** drilled by the rigs and flows through pipelines laid along the sea bed to the shore.

Life on an oil rig is tough and dangerous. Violent storms blow up, and the waves may reach heights of 30 metres. Sometimes the crews have to be taken off by helicopter, each man being hauled aboard on a rope as the helicopter hovers above the rig, for it is too risky to land in high winds. But the crews think the risks are worth taking. These brave men are bringing new riches to the countries that surround the North Sea.

Underground Cities

A **pithead** gives no indication of the size of a mine. It may look busy, as people bustle about among the buildings and trains clatter in and out to take away the coal. But beneath ground there is far more activity. If you could see the whole of a coal mine, it would look like an underground city.

Great **shafts** lead down from the pithead. They contain lifts to carry the miners to and from their work and to bring up the coal. Other smaller shafts let air into the mine. From these shafts great networks of **horizontal** tunnels lead out. These follow the **veins** of coal and may run many kilometres from the pithead. In some mines near the coast the tunnels extend under the sea.

Trains of wagons or **conveyor belts** run along the tunnels to transport the coal from the coal faces where the miners work. The men use cutting machines to get out the coal. Often holes are drilled into the rock and explosives used to blast out the coal. Here and there are rooms. The underground manager has an office, and a machine room contains electric fans to keep air circulating through the mine.

Every year miners dig out about 3000 million tonnes of coal in the world's mines. Coal mining is dirty work, but the pithead contains baths so that the miners can return home as clean as if they worked in an office. Coal mining is sometimes dangerous and coal dust can damage a miner's health. But miners are proud of the important work they do.

Right: *Inside a mine; a view of the shafts and tunnels below the surface.* **Inset and below:** *A machine which cuts into the coal-face as it moves along a track.*

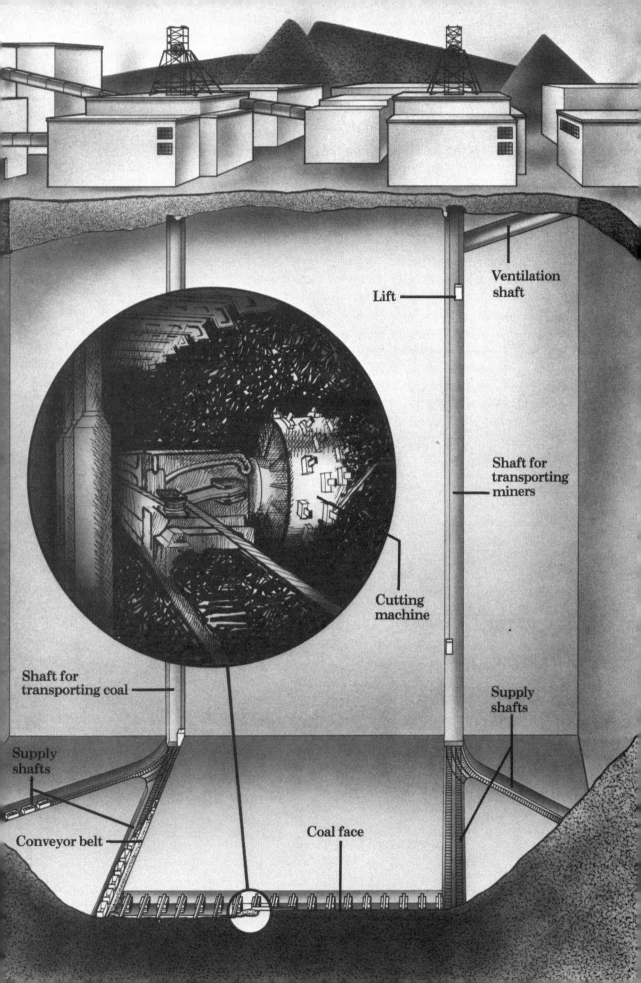

Ventilation
shaft

Lift

Shaft for
transporting
miners

Cutting
machine

Shaft for
transporting coal

Supply
shafts

Supply
shafts

Conveyor belt

Coal face

HAND-MADE
WORLD

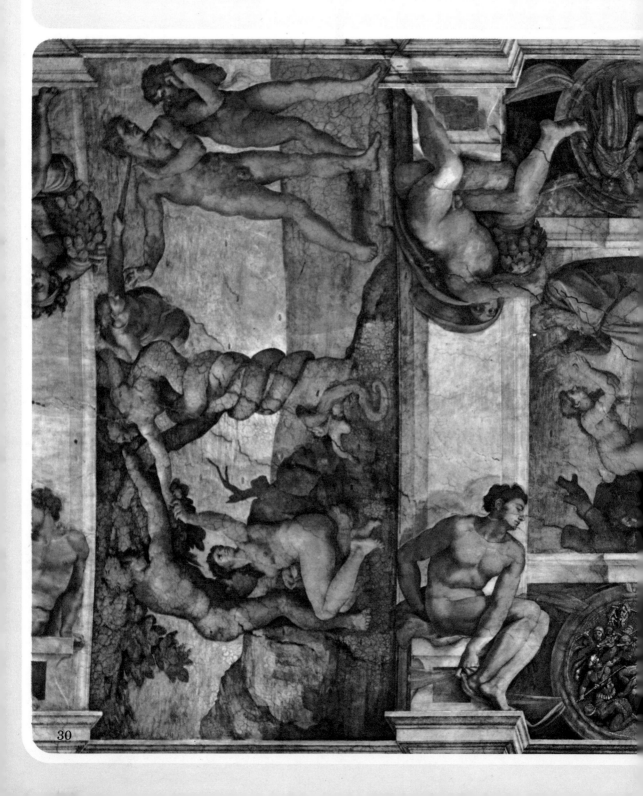

Man is different from other animals because he can make things for their beauty alone. For example he paints pictures in rich colours, carves magnificent shapes from rock and builds breathtaking structures just because they are pleasing to look at. The Italian artist Michelangelo worked single-handed for four years, lying uncomfortably on his back, to paint the magnificent ceiling of the Sistine Chapel in Rome, shown below.

The Hanging Stones

On Salisbury Plain in the part of southern England known as Wiltshire stands a strange monument that even the mighty Romans feared. Rings of great stones as tall as seven metres and weighing 45 tonnes tower high into the air. Some support other stones and form high arches. This is Stonehenge, an ancient name meaning 'hanging stones'. The Romans probably thought that only giants could have built such a place. They thought it was evil and deliberately destroyed as much of it as they were able to.

In time, many of the stones have fallen down and others have been broken up and used by farmers through the centuries to build homes for themselves and their animals. But on a cold, windswept day at Stonehenge, you can still sense among the ruins a little of the fear that the Romans felt.

Above: *One of the few arches remaining at Stonehenge. It is seven metres high and the lintel weighs seven tonnes.*
Left: *The 45 tonne standing stones at Stonehenge were hauled to the site on wooden sleds, and erected by tipping the base of the stone into a hole and then levering it up into position.*

The first stones were put up about 4,000 years ago, and they may even have been brought there from mountains in Wales 200 kilometres away. No one knows exactly how this was done. Some people think that each stone was slung by ropes between two boats and carried across the sea and up rivers. Or maybe the stones were tied to sledges and dragged across the land. One **legend** says that the wizard Merlin moved the stones by magic.

Many years later, the biggest stones were hauled from **quarries** only 40 kilometres away. The stone arches were built of these stones, and they formed an almost perfect circle around the earlier stones. The stones were carefully carved so that they fitted exactly.

Stonehenge is unique—this means there is no other monument like it anywhere else in the world. Why it was built is unknown, but it stands at the centre of a group of ancient burial mounds and prehistoric sites. It was probably therefore a great temple.

Right: *A view of Stonehenge as it was originally built. The lintels were placed on top of the standing stones by piling logs beneath them and slowly raising them into the air.*
Below: *Stonehenge as it appears today.*

Paintings from the Past

One day in 1940, a boy slithered into a hole on a scrubby hilltop at Lascaux in south-west France, trying to rescue a dog that had fallen down the hole. As his eyes became accustomed to the dark, the boy realized he had entered a cave, and on the walls of the cave were wonderful colourful paintings of hunting scenes, although the animals were not like any he knew. He had discovered paintings made by prehistoric men about 20,000 years ago. At that time the Ice Age was at its height, and that part of France was like the far north is today.

Below: *Stone Age man paints the walls of a cave with only the light of a small fire to help him while he creates his mysterious pictures.*

The paintings showed animals that now live only near the Arctic, such as reindeer and bison. The Lascaux cave is now closed, because the thousands of visitors have affected the paintings. But other cave paintings may be seen nearby. They show mammoths and woolly rhinoceroses, which are now extinct. Good cave paintings can also be seen at Altamira in north-east Spain.

The cavemen used red, yellow and brown paints made by grinding minerals into powder and mixing the powder with water. Black paint was made from soot or charcoal. Then the paint was daubed onto the rock walls of the caves with the fingers or with brushes or pads. The paintings are deep inside caves, often in the dark, and an open fire was used to give light. By painting a hunting scene the hunters may have thought this would bring them success in the next hunt for animals.

Giant Heads of Rock

Famous people are often remembered by carvings of their heads in stone or bronze that are mounted on a **plinth**. The heads are usually life-size, but two famous groups of carved heads exist that are gigantic. The first set of heads stare out in majesty; the second in mystery.

In 1927, John Borglum began a project to celebrate the greatness of the United States in a simple but breathtaking way. He climbed Mount Rushmore in South Dakota and started to carve the first of four heads from a granite cliff 150 metres high. He chose the presidents he most admired—George Washington, Abraham Lincoln, Thomas Jefferson and Theodore Roosevelt.

Above: *The four American presidents carved out of Mount Rushmore; from left to right, Washington, Jefferson, Roosevelt and Lincoln.*
Right: *One of the many carved heads, weighing up to 50 tonnes, to be found on Easter Island in the Pacific Ocean.*

Each head is between 18 and 20 metres high. They were declared an American National Memorial in 1929 and finished by Borglum's son Lincoln in 1941.

The second group of heads are totally different. Far away in the Pacific Ocean, a Dutch explorer landed on an unknown island on Easter Day, 1722, and he named it Easter Island. It is small, bare and rocky and in no way unusual—except for one thing. Near the shore are hundreds of carved heads standing in rows. Each head is ten or more metres high and capped with what looks like a hat or wig of red **volcanic rock**.

The heads were quarried from a volcanic crater and were made hundreds of years ago by people of whom little is known. Why they were built remains a mystery.

The Gold Mask

In 1922 one of the greatest finds of the ancient world was made. After many years of searching in the hot Egyptian desert, the British archaeologist Howard Carter finally discovered the tomb of King Tutankhamun. Many tombs of the ancient kings of Egypt had been found before, but robbers had removed their riches. The location of Tutankhamun's tomb was unknown, and its treasures lay undisturbed inside.

On 26 November Carter entered the tomb. Everywhere he saw the glint of gold, and he realized that

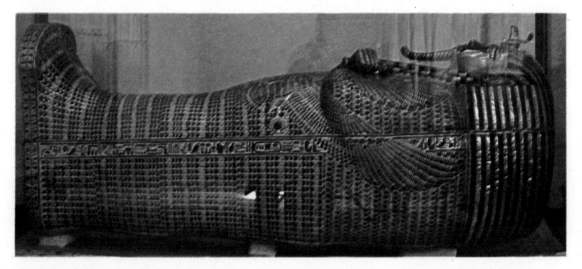

he was the first person of the modern world to look upon the full glory of an Egyptian king's tomb. All kinds of marvels lay before him: elegant furniture, statues, jewellery and shrines to help the king through the afterlife that the Egyptians believed awaited him after death. But the most exciting discovery was to come.

In an inner chamber Carter found the gold-covered coffin of Tutankhamun. Inside was another gold-covered coffin and inside that, a third coffin of solid gold. On opening this coffin he gazed upon the face of the king. It was not his real face, but that of a magnificent gold mask. The body of the young king—he was only about 18 years old when he died—lay encased in cloth, but over his head and shoulders was the mask. Made of **burnished gold** and decorated with the blue stone lapis lazuli and blue glass, it portrayed the boy king as a god. In this way he would become ruler of the dead.

Carter and his team spent ten years carefully removing the treasures from the tomb. Most of them are now housed in the Cairo Museum in Egypt.

Right: *The priceless death mask.* **Above:** *The magnificent coffin inside which the body of Tutankhamun rested for more than 3,000 years. The boy pharaoh only ruled Egypt for about ten years, 1361 to 1351 B.C., but the discovery of his tomb, one of the few to have survived, has put him among the most famous pharaohs. Many of the tombs that have been discovered up till now had nearly all their treasures stolen from them.*

Art from Rubbish

In Watts, a **suburb** of Los Angeles in the United States, stands one of the strangest monuments ever erected by man. Elegant towers rise into the air—not regular columns but odd-shaped frameworks of metal. Around them stand walls in multi-coloured patterns. The monument is known as Watts Towers, and it has no particular purpose. It was built by a man simply because he wanted to build it.

Simon Rodia came from Italy to the United States at the age of 12. He worked as a repairman and, at the age of 42, decided to build a monument in his back garden. 'I had in mind to do something big and I did,' he said later. 'You have to be good good or bad bad to be remembered.' Rodia had little money and so built his towers of whatever he could find or was given. Pieces of wire and steel rods, bits of broken tile or pottery, coloured glass, sea shells and cement—almost anything could somehow be used. Gradually the towers took shape.

Rodia finished them in 1954, when he was 75 years old. His task had taken him 33 years. He did not sit back to enjoy his creation, but left it to others to wonder at the towers. Rodia gave them, together with his house and

Opposite page: *A general view of Watts Towers in Los Angeles, California, U.S.A.*
Above: *The towers are made out of any kind of rubbish their creator, Simon Rodia, could get his hands on.*
Left: *Simon Rodia's initials can be seen making part of the pattern on the wall.*

garden, to a neighbour and left.

The city authorities were worried that the towers were unsafe: after all, they looked as if they had been put up any old how. But the towers were found to be enormously strong. Simon Rodia's strange structures stand in Los Angeles, California, as a monument to today's throwaway society—created from what most of us would consider to be worthless rubbish.

Patterns in the Desert

Anyone flying over the desert of southern Peru will not see sand dunes like the Sahara, but a flat expanse of dry brown earth stretching far away until it is broken by a line of stony hills on the distant horizon.

Suddenly you would see that the plain is covered with a mass of pale, sandy-coloured lines standing out against the dark earth. Huge triangles, squares and rectangles many kilometres across are linked with other curved shapes. A whirling spiral forms the tail of a monkey and there are enormous drawings of all kinds of creatures from a spider to a long-legged dog. Each of these vast, mysterious drawings is made from one unbroken line.

Right: *Some of the Nazca lines run straight for many kilometres over the stony desert and across the Peruvian mountains. Nobody knows why they are there or how anybody, 2,000 years ago, could have made them.*

Above: *Other Nazca lines form huge patterns and pictures, this monkey's paw is 12 metres across. These pictures can only be seen from the air.*

A closer look shows that the lines are, in fact, shallow grooves in the surface of the desert made by sweeping away the dark topsoil and revealing paler earth beneath. Some of the lines are no more than a metre across. Others, wide enough to drive a car along, stretch many kilometres across the desert.

It is thought that the patterns were drawn by the Nazca people who lived in Peru about 2,000 years ago. They were mostly farmers and probably used the mysterious drawings as some form of calendar.

Town in a nutshell

Just a short tramride from the centre of The Hague, a big city in Holland, is a town where even the smallest person can feel like a giant. You can stroll along its streets and canals with their beautiful old houses, as it is a typical Dutch town. But if you want to look inside them you would have to get down on your hands and knees. For this is Madurodam, a model town where everything is one-twenty-fifth of its real size. You tower over the buildings and marvel at the way every little detail is there, but so much smaller than its true size.

There are the buildings you would find in any town—churches, theatres, stores, schools and factories—as well as docks and an airport. But there are also important buildings, several of them exact **replicas** of famous buildings in The Hague. You would even see an oil-tanker on fire.

Right: *A child walks among the miniature buildings of the model town of Madurodam in Holland.*
Opposite page: *The market place of Madurodam.*

As you look down on the town, feeling rather like Gulliver among the little people of Lilliput, you become aware that this is not just a dead, lifeless model. Trains rush along the railways; a lively fair is in full swing; a procession with a golden coach is entering the Parliament buildings accompanied by a military band that is actually playing; and you can also hear the strange sound of the old barrel organ, which is still to be seen and heard in Holland today.

Madurodam becomes even more magical at night. As dusk falls, the many thousands of lights in the town come on, and you can really imagine yourself to be a real inhabitant of this amazing little city. Since it was opened in 1952, Madurodam has been visited by more than 20 million people. And each person walks two miles round the town. More than one million people come to Madurodam every year.

Jigsaw Pictures

Few of the paintings of ancient people have lasted to our time, but whenever an ancient **villa** is discovered, a mosaic is almost sure to be found. These ancient mosaics usually decorated the floors of homes and temples.

Mosaics are pictures made from small pieces of coloured stone, tile or glass. They are made simply by pressing the pieces of coloured stone, tile or glass into cement. Seen from a distance, the mosaic figures and scenes look very lifelike.

It is possible, especially in Greece and Italy, to visit

Above: *A wall mosaic from San Vitale, Ravenna in Italy, showing the Byzantine Emperor Justinian and his courtiers. This mosaic was made about 547 A.D.* **Right:** *Mosaics are created by pressing small squares of coloured material into cement.*

ruins and see mosaic floors and pavements in as good a condition as when they were first laid. But many of the best mosaics have been taken from their original sites and put into museums. A large mosaic, now in the British Museum, was discovered only a few years ago in a field in Dorset when a farm worker was digging a hole. There are probably many more beautiful mosaics lying undiscovered beneath the ground in the countries that used to be the Roman Empire.

Among the most superb mosaics are those of religious figures that cover the walls and ceilings of Byzantine churches in Italy and Greece.

47

Crystal Skull

The human skull has long been a reminder of death. In 1809, in Yugoslavia, the Turks built a tower containing nearly a thousand skulls of captured **rebels** to frighten the people of the Serbian lands into obeying them. Pirates displayed a skull and crossbones on their flags to strike terror into their captives. The skull and crossbones is still used as a sign of death, but more to warn people of danger rather than to scare them. For example, containers of poison carry such a marking.

This beautiful crystal skull was carved from rock crystal by an Aztec craftsman. The Aztecs were no strangers to death. In fact it formed a central part of their religion. The Aztecs believed that many of their gods could only be pleased by human **sacrifice**. They thought, too, that human sacrifice would induce the gods to make the land fertile. And, without implements such as the wheel to make work easier, life was hard, so it is not surprising that the gods were cruel. The **victims**, who were sacrificed in the temples, were usually captured enemies. When the Spanish **conquistadores** arrived in Mexico about 450 years ago, they found many tribes willing to help them defeat the Aztecs.

Right: *The crystal skull was made by an Aztec craftsman. The Aztec people ruled much of the land now called Mexico until the Spanish conquistadores arrived 450 years ago.*

The craftsmanship displayed in the crystal skull is very impressive. Much time and great trouble has been taken to smooth and polish the rock so that it shines brilliantly. In size it is slightly smaller than a real skull. The origins of the skull are unknown. It was thought to have been made before Christopher Columbus reached America in 1492. However, recent tests show that the lines forming the teeth may have been made with a small cutting wheel. In this case the skull must have been made later, because the wheel was unknown in America before the Spaniards arrived. The skull can now be seen in the British Museum in London.

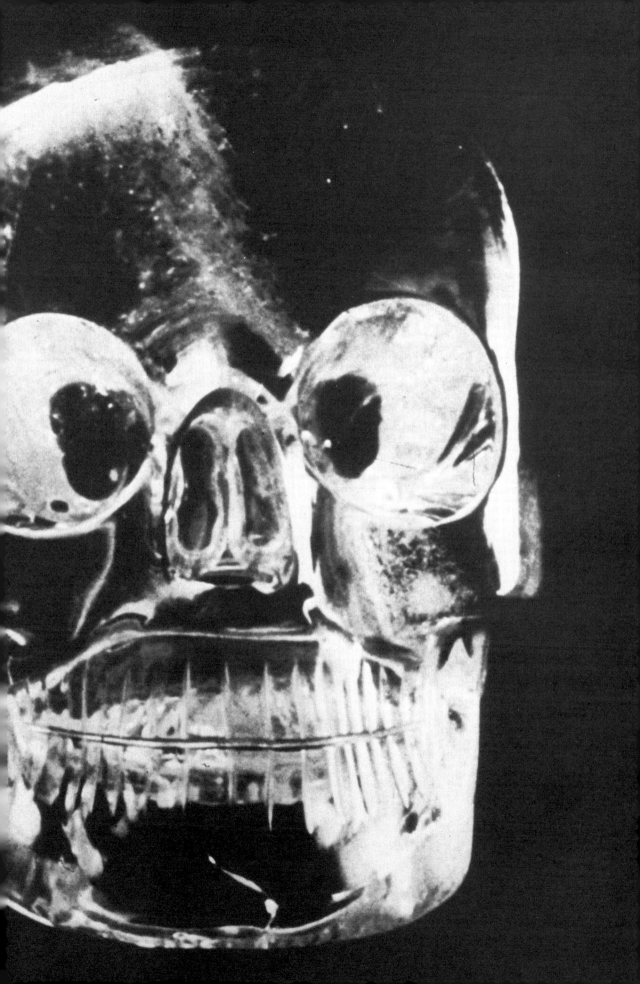

CHANGING THE FACE OF OUR WORLD

From the beginning of man's history on Earth he has changed his surroundings to suit himself—a smooth road over rough ground, strong bridges to cross rivers and gaping chasms and vast areas of fertile land where there was once desert.

As man's knowledge and ability increased so did the size of projects he undertook—from the early Roman road builders we have now progressed to being able to build the highly complex Spaghetti Junction in Birmingham, England, that you can see below.

Ribbons of Concrete

Every country needs a system of roads and railways just as the body needs arteries and veins to carry life-giving blood to its every part. Goods must move to and fro and keep people in work, and the people themselves must travel and meet one another. Since 1926, when Germany began to build the first motorways, other countries have developed their road transport instead of railways. Now many countries have long ribbons of motorways winding through their countryside, **bypassing** cities.

As road building has grown, new machines for laying roads have been invented. Many new roads are made of concrete, and many more roads are being laid by a huge machine known as a Slip Form Paver.

The base of the road is first prepared and made strong enough to take the weight of the paving machine. Then wires or cords are positioned along the road to guide the machine. The paver automatically follows the wires as concrete is fed into it. Two other machines follow the paver over the newly-laid concrete. One of these machines makes joints in the concrete to allow the road to move slightly in order to take the weight of fast-moving lorries and cars—without these joints the road would eventually break up. The last machine makes grooves in the soft concrete with wire brushes and coats it with a fine skin of polyethylene which forms the final road surface. The machines work fast, making one and a half metres of road every minute!

Motorway accidents are rare, but when they do happen they are bad because the traffic travels at such high speeds. For complete safety, future motorways may be built with guidance systems, and every vehicle's speed and direction will be electronically controlled.

Above: *Building a concrete highway using a Slip Form Paver, a huge road-making machine.*

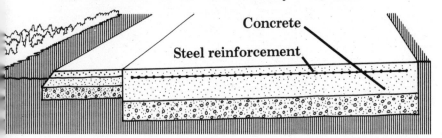

Concrete

Steel reinforcement

Above: *A concrete highway consists of layers of concrete laid over a base of stones. The concrete may be reinforced by placing steel cables in it. The cables pull the concrete together, giving it extra strength. Reinforced concrete is also used in constructing buildings.*

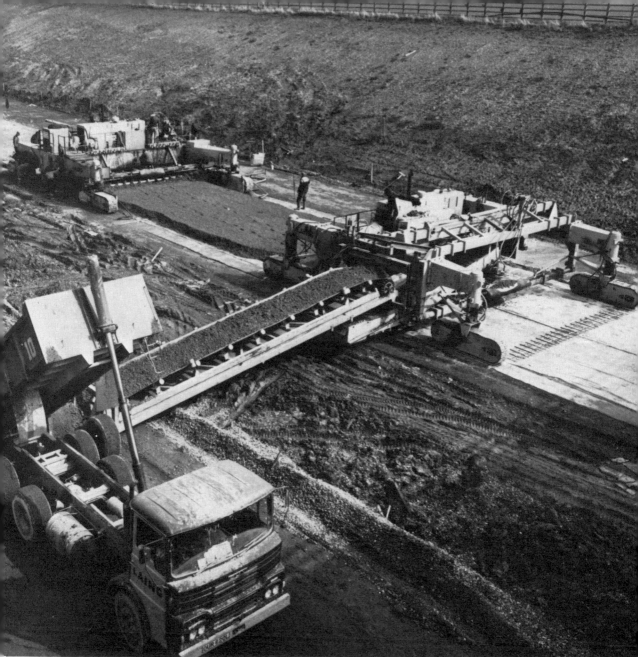

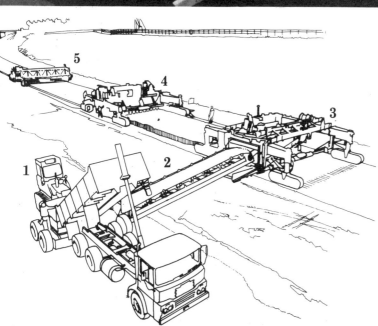

Left: *The road is made by first feeding concrete (1) from a lorry along a conveyor belt (2) to the Slip Form Paver. The paver spreads the concrete (3) and compacts it to form the road (4). Another machine prepares the final surface (5).*

The Road Builders

What is it like to make a journey on a motorway? It can be thrilling because you can go fast and the road seems to go on for ever. There are never any towns to slow you down but you can stop at the service stations to stretch your legs, get a meal or fill up the car with petrol

If you were a wealthy Roman living about two thousand years ago, you could say the same things about the marvellous roads that crossed the Roman Empire. Instead of a car, you would travel in a two-wheeled chariot drawn by a team of horses and you would change your horses instead of filling up with petrol.

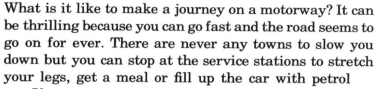

Stone flags

Gravel

Concrete

Stony layer

Compacted earth

You could go almost anywhere, for the Roman Empire contained 85,000 kilometres of roads. The roads were large—up to ten metres wide—and some had separate lanes for chariots and wagons which moved at different speeds. Wherever possible, Roman roads were completely straight so that a journey could be made as quickly as possible. Like a motorway, they did not bend to avoid obstacles. The roads often ran from one military camp to another and avoided towns.

Every 40 kilometres (about the same distance apart as the service stations on a motorway), there was a rest house. Here you could have a meal and stay overnight. In between rest houses, there were horse-changing stations where a small inn offered refreshments to travellers.

The Romans built their roads so that their armies could march rapidly from one part of the Roman Empire to another. Travellers in a hurry could cover as much as 300 kilometres in 24 hours, although such a speed was exceptional. Even today few motorists like to drive more than twice this distance in a day.

Small stretches of Roman road can still be seen. If you look at a road map, you will see some long stretches of older roads (not motorways) that are totally straight.

Opposite page: *Roman roads were made of layers of stones often a metre or more deep, with curbs at the sides to hold in the stones, and ditches to carry away rain water.*

Above: *Watling Street in England is a good example of the long straight roads built by the Romans, and is still in use today.*

Left: *Because roads became very muddy, the Romans built stepping stones with spaces between them for horses and chariot wheels.*

55

Man-made Rivers

Every town needs a supply of water. However, not all towns are built near water. Many towns were built on high ground away from the marshy land at the bottom of valleys. On high ground they could be better defended from enemies. Wells were dug to get water, but often extra water had to be brought in from outside the town.

A distant river was the source and water was carried along a channel to the town. The channel had to be built sloping downwards slightly so that the water would flow easily. Where the channel came to a valley, a bridge had to be built to carry the channel across the valley. Such a bridge is called an aqueduct, and it may be a **canal** as well as a supply of water.

There are records of large canal and aqueduct systems being in existence during the reign of Rameses

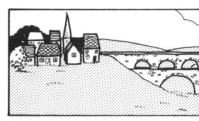

Above: *An aqueduct leads water over a valley to a town.*

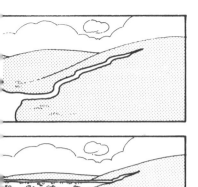

II in the 14th century B.C. The earliest known aqueducts in Europe were built around 625 B.C. in Greece. Many magnificent aqueducts were built by the Romans to supply their cities and towns with water. Most of these no longer exist or are in ruins, but several still stand. The best in Europe is the aqueduct at Segovia in Spain, and the one shown below, which is near Nîmes in southern France.

Nîmes got its water from a source 50 kilometres away, and this aqueduct was built in 19 B.C., nearly 2,000 years ago, to carry water across the River Gardon. The aqueduct is called the Pont du Gard, and its three layers of arches rise 49 metres above the river. It is best seen in the evening, when its golden stone glows in the light of the setting sun. It is possible to walk along the top, which is 275 metres long, for water no longer flows along the famous aqueduct.

Below: *The Pont du Gard near Nîmes in southern France.*

Spanning Great Rivers

From the shore, a modern suspension bridge seems to soar effortlessly across a wide river or channel. It seems to be held up by two flimsy lines strung between high towers at each end. A close look shows that the flimsy lines are thick cables of great strength. And at each end of the bridge the cables are buried deep in the ground to hold up the bridge.

The longest bridges are suspension bridges because wire for making cables is strong and a vast span can be built without any central support going into the water. So nothing gets in the way of ships and boats. Also, suspension bridges can be built high across a wide **gorge** or **chasm**.

The longest span of any bridge is that of the

Below: The Golden Gate Bridge at San Francisco spans the entrance to the harbour.

Opposite page: The world's longest single span bridge—the Verrazano Narrows Bridge, stretching across the entrance to New York City Harbour, USA. The picture shows the huge cables that support the bridge being made from thousands of strands of wire. The bridge has two levels.

Verrazano Narrows Bridge, a suspension bridge at the entrance of New York harbour in the United States of America. The central span is 1298 metres long. The bridge is so long that it has to curve slightly because of the **curvature** of the Earth. However, a suspension bridge with a central span of 1410 metres over the River Humber in England will be the longest when it is finished in 1978. It will have the longest span for only ten years, after which a suspension bridge with a central span 1780 metres long will open in Japan.

Suspension bridges are not new. For many centuries primitive people have been making rope bridges across **ravines**. The bridges were made of three ropes—one to walk on and one on each side to grip with the hands.

The Mole

One important kind of engineering work is carried out without changing the face of the Earth, and this is tunnelling. Tunnels have to be cut through mountain ranges and under rivers and channels to allow road and rail traffic to travel quickly from one side to the other. Water tunnels have to be dug to take water from dams. Tunnels beneath cities carry underground railways and roadways.

Although they are surrounded by solid rock, the engineers must know exactly where they are so that the tunnel will be in the correct place. Often a tunnel is begun at both ends and the two tunnelling teams meet in the middle if their **calculations** are correct! They always are, and to within a few centimetres. But sometimes a small tunnel is bored first and then made larger into a full-scale tunnel.

Digging a tunnel can be a dangerous job. Sometimes there are rock falls and accidents happen. During the building of the world's longest railway tunnel—the 20-kilometre Simplon II tunnel under the Alps—60 lives were lost. But this was over 50 years ago, and now

Above: *French and Italian tunnellers meet in the middle of the massive Mont Blanc tunnel.*

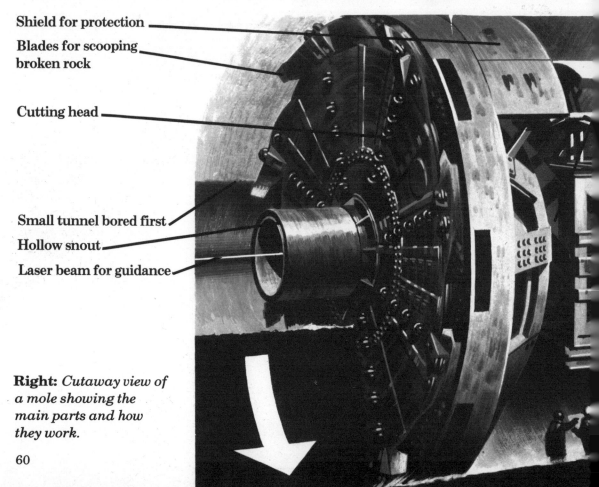

Shield for protection

Blades for scooping broken rock

Cutting head

Small tunnel bored first

Hollow snout

Laser beam for guidance

Right: *Cutaway view of a mole showing the main parts and how they work.*

tunnellers have the help of the mechanical mole.

The mechanical mole is an extraordinary machine which does all the digging, and seems to eat its way through the rock. At its head are many electrically-powered cutting blades that break up the rock. The broken pieces are scooped up by **rotating** blades and emptied into a **chute**, and then carried away back down the tunnel on a **conveyor belt**. The mole has an automatic (laser beam) guidance system, which makes sure that it digs the correct path for the tunnel. The machine pushes itself into the rock with powerful **hydraulic** arms that grip the sides of the tunnel. As it moves forward, lining segments are fixed in place to line the tunnel and stop any rock falling in. Tunnelling with the mechanical mole is safe and only needs about 20 men to work it. It is also very fast: in 1967 a three metre wide tunnel was lengthened by 114 metres in just one day.

Chute   Lining segments   Hydraulic arms   Conveyor belt

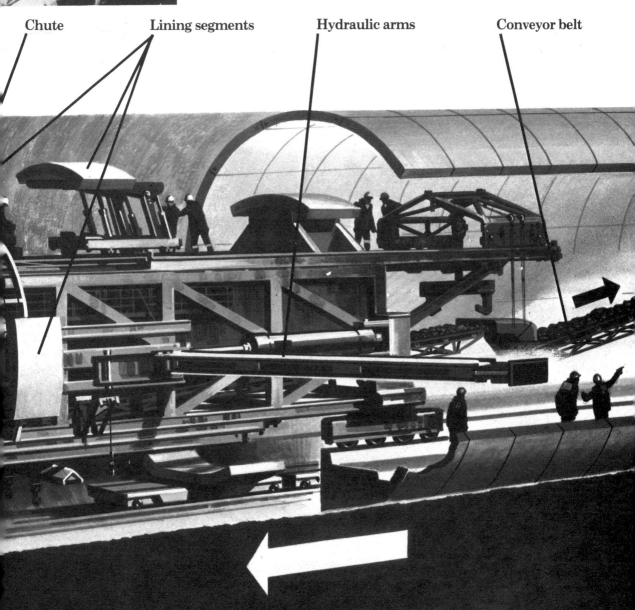

Linking the Oceans

There are several places in the world where great seas and oceans are only kept apart by a very narrow strip of land. In Greece, the Gulf of Corinth is separated from the Aegean Sea by a narrow strip of land only six kilometres wide. The Red Sea stretches an arm of water—the Gulf of Suez—towards the Mediterranean Sea, and fails to reach

Opposite page: *A ship passes through a lock on the Panama Canal.* **Right:** *A lock separates two sections of a canal or river that are at different levels. To raise itself a boat enters the lower lock gate (1) which then closes. A sluice opens in the upper gate (2) and raises the water level in the lock to the higher level. Finally (3) the upper gate opens and the boat sails on.*

it by about a 160 kilometres.

The most spectacular of these narrow strips of land is that of Panama. There, only 80 kilometres of land separate the Atlantic Ocean from the Pacific Ocean. In the past sailors looked longingly at the sea or ocean separated from them only by this strip of land, knowing that if this land was water it would save them a long voyage. So man has carved great canals across these tongues of land to shorten ocean voyages.

The Suez Canal was opened in 1869. At long last ships sailing between Europe and the East did not have to make the long voyage around Africa. The Corinth Canal followed in 1893, slicing its way in a deep straight gash through the rock in southern Greece. In 1914 came the Panama Canal, winding its way up and down through locks to link the world's two greatest oceans. It not only cuts as much as 12,000 kilometres off voyages, but saves ships from having to sail through the hazardous waters off Cape Horn.

Land from the Sea

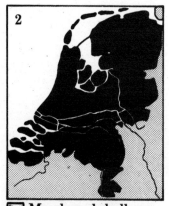

Above: *Holland as it looked in the first century AD.*

Marsh and shallows
Habitable land
Above: *Holland today.*
Below: *The barrages of the Delta Project contain culverts to allow fish to pass through.*

The country of Holland is also known as The Netherlands, which means low lands. It is a very good name, because a quarter of the country lies below sea level. Two thousand years ago this land was covered with marsh and often flooded as high tides and storms forced the sea inland. But the Dutch people long ago decided to fight the sea. They set about building barriers called **dykes** to keep out the sea. They made windmills to pump out the water and dug canals to take it away. Gradually, Holland began to look as it does today—a land of flat plains crisscrossed by canals and dotted with windmills.

In this century, the Dutch have begun two huge projects to push back the sea even farther and so get more land. Several centuries ago the North Sea broke into Holland and flooded a huge central area, making an inland sea called the Zuider Zee. In 1923, a barrier was built across it to hold back the sea. This turned the Zuider Zee into a great freshwater lake now called the IJssel Meer. Then great areas of land called **polders** were reclaimed by surrounding them with dykes and pumping out the water. This project will be finished by 1978 after more than 50 years' work! But Holland will have obtained more than 2500 square kilometres of land from the sea. Once the minerals and salts are removed, the land will be suitable for farming.

In 1953, great storms caused very heavy floods in southern Holland as the sea overflowed river **estuaries**. Nearly 2,000 people were drowned. To stop such loss of life and to prevent the sea water ruining farming land, the Delta Project was born. When it is finished in 1978, the estuaries will be sealed off by great dams. Roads will run across the dams, and there will be freshwater lakes behind them. The sea at long last will have been tamed.

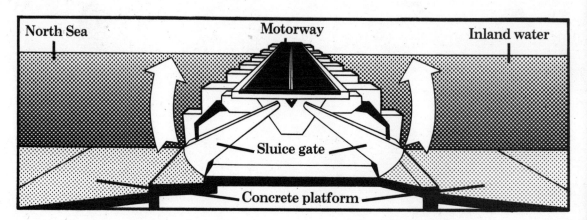

North Sea   Motorway   Inland water

Sluice gate

Concrete platform

Right: *To make one of the barrages in the Delta Project, an artificial island was first constructed in an estuary. Then the barrage was built on the island.*
Below: *When completed, the island was destroyed and the barrage stood ready to hold back the sea.*

Giant Staircases

Nowhere has man changed the face of the Earth more dramatically than in the rice-growing countries of southern Asia. These lands have so many people that every available piece of ground is used to grow rice. In upland regions, people have carved out terraces on the hillsides and along steep valleys, covering the slopes with what look like giant staircases of bright green. The people have little help from machines. They have dug out row upon row of terraces with only simple tools.

Terracing has two purposes. Most varieties of rice grow best in flooded or very damp ground. The flat terraces will hold water that would otherwise run off the hillside. But terracing also helps farming in general because it stops rainwater from carrying away particles of soil as it runs downhill. Without terracing, hillsides gradually lose their **fertile** soil and **crops** will not grow. Also, it is difficult to **harvest** crops on sloping land.

The flooded rice fields are called paddies. The level of the water is controlled by building low walls of earth. As

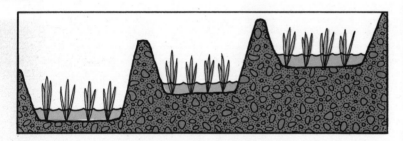

Above: *Low walls of earth keep the water in the field, around the growing rice.*
Opposite page: *Rice terraces cover the sides and floor of a steep valley in the Philippines.*

the young shoots of rice grow, the water level is raised to keep the roots well supplied with water. At this stage the paddies are bright green. As the rice ripens, it takes on a golden colour and the water level is lowered. By harvest time the fields are drained of water.

Half the people in the world have rice as their main food and most of it is produced in the Far East. China is the world's largest producer, growing more than 100 million tonnes a year. The rice that is eaten in many western countries has had most of its goodness removed to make it look white and shiny. If the people who live only on rice eat this type, they can become ill.

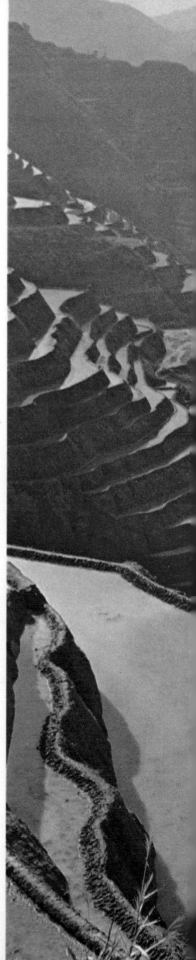

Turning Deserts into Orchards

There are many places in the world where **crops** will not grow. The North and South Poles are too cold, parts of the tropics are too wet, and the deserts are too dry. There are also many places where people have ruined the land. This has happened because they have cut down forests

Right: *Before and after a canal brings water to the land.*
Opposite page: *A desert that is being changed into fertile land.*
Inset: *The results of overgrazing.*

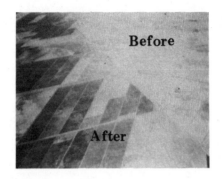

Before

After

and allowed animals such as goats to graze on the land until they have eaten away all the plants. The roots of the plants hold the soil together, and when they are gone the wind and rain loosen the soil and begin to blow or wash it away. Soon, all life has gone and a bare landscape is all that is left where **fertile land** used to be.

This spoiling of the land is called **soil erosion.** Once it starts, it can get worse very quickly. Most of the United States has been farmed for only about a hundred years, but five per cent of its land has been completely ruined by soil erosion. Now farmers in many countries know about soil erosion, and try to stop it happening. But other farmers still do not realize that their ways of farming are ruining the land.

However, it is now possible to bring spoilt land and dry desert land to life. By careful planting of grasses, shrubs and trees and replacing the top soil if necessary, spoilt land can become fertile and grow plants again. Irrigation canals have been built to take water from **reservoirs** and lakes to the edges of deserts, where crops will grow easily in the sunshine if they have water.

The deserts of southern Israel have been changed into orchards and fields by bringing water in concrete-lined canals from lakes at the other end of the country. Using nuclear power (you can read about nuclear power on pages 14, 15, 16 and 17), fresh water may one day be made from sea water. Irrigation canals will then take this water to the desert areas.

THE MANY WAYS OF TALKING

There are many reasons why man has been able to progress from being a savage to being civilized. One of the most important is our ability to talk to each other. Animals exchange only simple ideas among themselves. They can tell one another that danger is approaching, for example, but not exactly what kind of danger.

We can exchange complicated ideas between ourselves, and from one idea another idea is born, and then another and another. (The picture below is of a radio telescope in Bahrain.)

Listening to the Stars

An **astronomer** sitting in his **observatory,** peering through a telescope into the skies, is rather like a fish at the bottom of a pond trying to find out what lies beyond it. All kinds of things are happening outside, in the Universe, but special eyes and ears are needed to find out about them. Astronomers now have **satellites** working for them above the Earth's **atmosphere,** and on the ground they have great radio telescopes to capture the **radio signals** that reach us from the stars.

These telescopes have found out that the Universe

Opposite page: Radio telescopes consist of either one large dish-shaped aerial (left) or an array of smaller aerials (right). Below: The world's largest radio telescope at Arecibo, Puerto Rico. It is built into a natural valley.

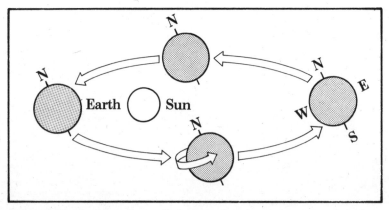

Above: *Because of the way the Earth travels around the Sun even an unsteerable telescope, such as Arecibo, can cover a wide area of the sky.*

probably started with a tremendous explosion some 10,000 million years ago. They have discovered strange things in the heavens, such as the mysterious quasars, which are very bright but seem to be very far away, and pulsars, which flash on and off all the time like the beam of a lighthouse. The great Arecibo radio telescope has been used to send radar signals to the planets and to capture the signals that bounce back. In this way the fact that Mercury and Venus rotate was discovered, and radar pictures have been made of the surface of Venus, which is always hidden beneath clouds.

The radio signals now leaving our planet must make it a great radio beacon in space. Radio telescopes have sent out special messages telling anyone who might be listening all about ourselves. These messages are now speeding out through space to the stars. Meanwhile, radio astronomers are also listening for any messages that might be coming from civilizations far out in space, but so far nothing understandable has been received.

Jodrell Bank

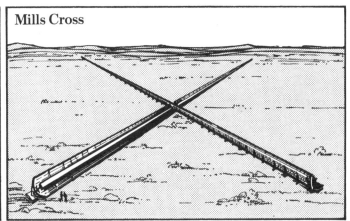

Mills Cross

Voices Around the World

Nowadays you can go to the telephone, dial as few as twelve numbers, and within seconds you can be speaking to someone on the other side of the world. And if an event of world-wide interest is taking place anywhere in the world, such as the Olympic Games, you will be able to watch it on television as it actually happens.

To be able to communicate instantly with any part of the world is one of the great benefits of spaceflight. Your telephone call goes through the telephone network to a transmitting station, which sends your voice (in the form

Opposite page: *A communications satellite in orbit high above the Atlantic Ocean directs telephone calls from one side of the ocean to the other.*

Right: *A satellite communications aerial sends out and picks up the telephone calls to and from the satellites in space. From the aerial, the calls received then travel to the telephone exchange.*

of a radio signal) thousands of kilometres up into space. There, high above the Earth, a communications satellite captures the signal and immediately sends it back down to Earth again to a receiving station in another country on the other side of the world. From this station the signal goes into the telephone network. The signals travel so fast that you cannot hear any delay as you talk over such a long distance. A single communications satellite can handle about 12,500 telephone calls at once.

Television signals are sent from one side of the world to the other by satellite in the same way as telephone signals. As many as twelve programmes can be transmitted at the same time through one satellite.

Many communications satellites are so high that they take exactly one day to go once around the Earth. The Earth turns beneath them as they travel, so they always appear to hang motionless in the very same place in the sky.

Before the development of the communications satellite cables had to be laid from country to country and continent to continent. The longest intercontinental cable yet laid is between Australia and Canada. It is 14,480 kilometres long and cost 35 million pounds to lay under the Pacific Ocean.

Pictures Through Space

One of the marvels of modern science comes into our homes. This is television and we can sit in front of a set and be entertained without moving a muscle. But the most exciting thing about television is that we can see what is going on all over the world—and the Universe—from our home. We can learn more and more about our world and how all its people live, and this should help to bring us all closer together. Spacecraft with television cameras can send us pictures from the Moon and from planets millions of kilometres away, opening up the Universe before our very eyes.

How does this miracle work? A television camera has a light-sensitive plate. The **image** of the scene before the camera goes through the lens and onto this plate. The plate turns the image into hundreds of **horizontal** lines. Each line is made of tiny dots of light, some bright, some dull. The dots are turned into **electric signals** and these signals are then changed into radio waves at the **transmitter**. The waves then travel through the air to the aerial in your home.

The aerial captures the waves and turns them back into electric signals. These pass into the television set, where they are changed into an electronic beam in the tube behind the screen. The beam is pointed at the screen and makes it glow with light. The beam moves across the screen from left to right, receiving the incoming signals and building up the picture dot by dot, line by line, many times a second. Our eyes combine these separate pictures to form a moving image, the same scene that the television camera has in front of it.

With colour television we see three images at once—one red, one green and one blue—which the eye puts together to form a full-colour picture.

Above: *A drama production in a television studio.*
Left: *The director in the control room tells the cameramen, through their headphones, what to do and also chooses which camera views to use in the final show.*

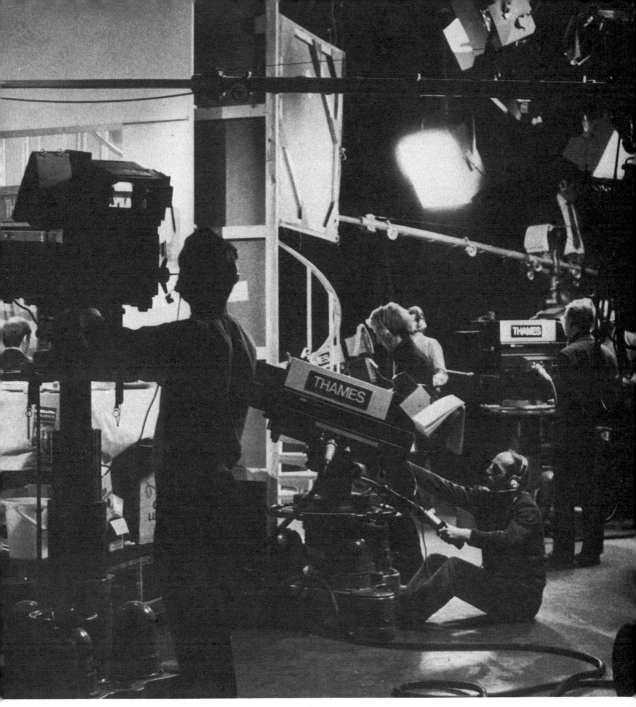

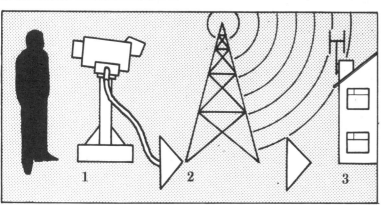

Left: *Television pictures are sent through the air in the form of radio signals. They start from the camera (1), then to the transmitter (2). They are picked up by an aerial on the building (3) which is connected to the television set.*

77

Magic Pictures

When photography was first invented, more than 150 years ago, a picture could only be taken with a large camera supported on a **tripod**. If the photographer wanted to take a picture outside, he had to carry a vast amount of equipment, including a tent that could be used as a dark-room to prepare the photographic plates! Modern cameras and films are much more convenient.

Now a new method of photography has been invented that seems to produce pictures by magic. With a camera called the Polaroid SX-70, all the photographer has to do is look through the viewfinder and turn a control to make the image he sees clear, and then press a

Above: *Although it is a highly advanced piece of equipment, the SX-70 is so simple to use that a person with no skill is sure to get a good result.*

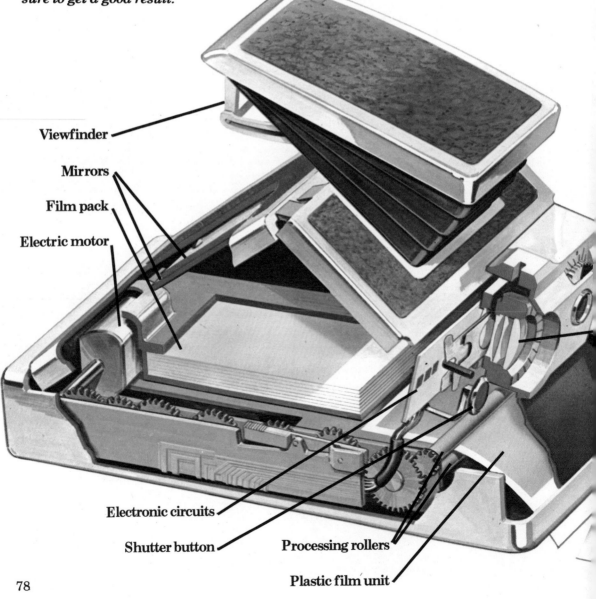

Viewfinder

Mirrors

Film pack

Electric motor

Electronic circuits

Shutter button

Processing rollers

Plastic film unit

button. Within two seconds a plastic card comes out of the camera and slowly changes into a colour picture of the scene the photographer has just looked at.

The camera does not have to be adjusted for the light and no developing is necessary. Everything is totally automatic. The SX-70 camera looks at the scene with an electric eye and measures the light reaching the camera. The electric eye operates **magnetic** controls that change the shutter speed and the **aperture** of the lens to the correct settings. Mirrors inside the camera send the image formed by the lens to the viewfinder, so that the photographer can see exactly what picture he is taking. As the shutter button is pressed, an electric motor moves the mirrors so that the image strikes a film pack. The film pack contains a set of plastic card-like film units and a wafer-thin battery. This battery powers the electric motor and the **electronic circuits** in the camera. There is a new battery in every film pack.

Immediately the image of the scene before the camera has flashed onto the top film unit in the pack, the motor pushes it out of the camera. As the film unit leaves, it goes through rollers and is squeezed so that small pods of **chemicals** in the layers of the film unit break open. A dye spreads over the film, acting like a curtain to stop light entering the inner layers. The colour of the dye slowly fades and in a few minutes the colour picture is ready.

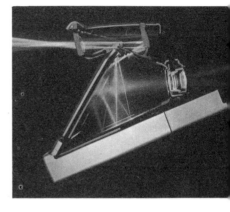

Above: *This shows how the beams of light strike the film pack and also go through the viewfinder.* **Below:** *The inside of an SX-70 showing how the motor drives the exposed film out of the camera. The different stages of developing can be seen on the right.*

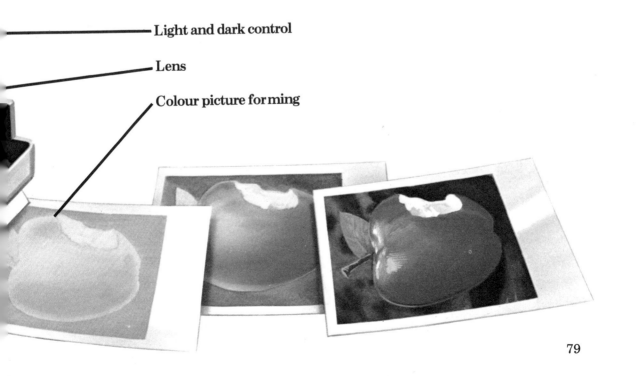

——————————————— Light and dark control

————————— Lens

—————— Colour picture forming

Until the invention of transistors, radios worked by valves. They were large and clumsy-looking devices which often broke down. The transistorized radios of today are much smaller, completely portable, have longer working lives without breakdown and are also inexpensive.

Bringing the World Alive

Nearly a hundred years ago, **scientists** discovered how to make new kinds of invisible rays—radio waves. These rays can travel across oceans and **continents,** and they can be made to carry messages. At first, **Morse signals** were **transmitted** and then speech and music. The whole world is now alive with radio.

If you take a radio and turn the tuning knob round as far as it will go, you should hear many stations come and go. Throughout the world radio is bringing news and entertainment to people. And there are other **radio channels** beyond the range of the normal radio. Directed by radio, a taxi, a service van—or possibly even a policeman—may be at your door in a matter of moments.

Ships at sea and aircraft depend on radio to find their way safely. You use radio waves if you make a long-distance telephone call that is helped by **satellite** (you can read about satellites on pages 74 and 75). Or you can talk directly to a friend hundreds or thousands of kilometres away with your own radio **transmitter** over the special **amateur** radio band.

Radio works by changing speech or music into **electric signals** and then turning the signals into radio waves. The waves travel through the air or through space to an aerial, where they are captured and turned back into electric signals. The radio set then changes the signals back into sound you can hear.

Right: *A valve is many times larger than a transistor, even though each does exactly the same job. Transistors were invented in 1948, and can now be made so small that they can hardly be seen. This is why televisions and radios can be very small.*

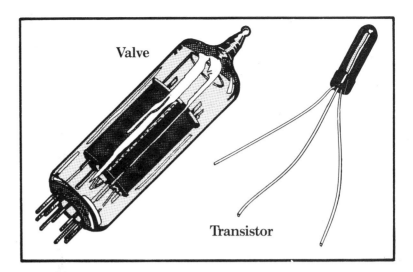

Valve

Transistor

Four Colours make a Rainbow

Many of the books we can buy nowadays have beautiful pictures in full colour. How do so many colours get on the paper? If we wanted to print a picture of a rainbow, would we have to print every colour separately with a different coloured ink? This method would work, but it would make books very expensive.

A painter does not need a complete range of colours to make a painting. Instead, he mixes a few basic colours together to get all the shades he wants. Colour printing works in the same way, and if you look at any of the colour pictures in this book under a magnifying glass, you will see that they are made up of dots of only four colours. When you take the magnifying glass away, the dots of colour appear so small to the eye that they mix together and make new colours. Pictures with all the colours of the rainbow can be printed in this way.

Right: *Four stages in the process of printing a full colour picture.*
1. The yellow filter picture.
2. The yellow filter with the magenta, or red, filter.
3. The yellow and magenta with the cyan, or blue, filter.
4. The final stage of printing with the three complementary colours and black. This gives us our full colour picture.

1

2

3

4

In fact only three colours are needed to make up all other colours. These three colours are known as complementary colours, and they are yellow, magenta (red-blue) and cyan (blue-green). Black is then added to make the picture life-like.

All colour photographs or drawings that are printed in this book have been placed in a special camera that photograph them in black and white four times—once for the black plate and then through different coloured filters of blue, yellow and red for the colour plates. It also splits the picture up into the tiny dots of colour. Four **printing plates** are made from these photographs. When the picture is being printed, the paper comes in contact with each of the printing plates in turn. First yellow, then the magenta over the top, then blue over that, and finally black on top of this. This order of printing the colours on top of each other can change, but usually the black plate is printed last.

Below: *A part of picture 4 enlarged many times to show the tiny dots, or screens. When they are seen at the right size they give us the impression of full colour.*

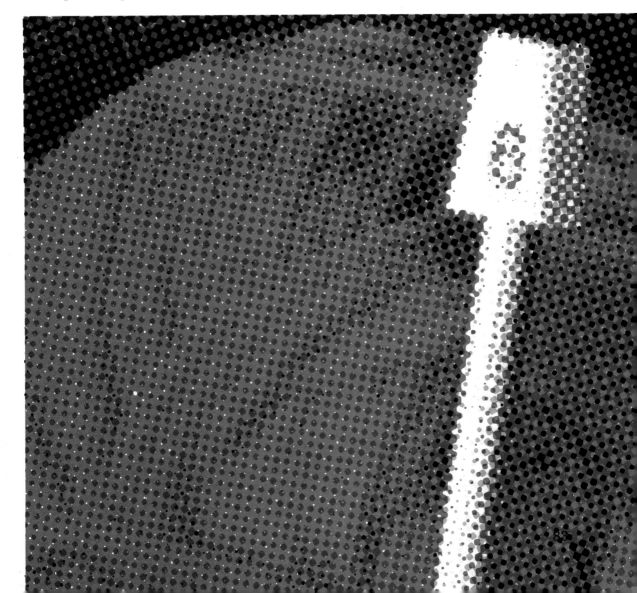

When Seeing is not Believing

In real life, we know that something is true because we see it with our own eyes. But we should not always believe our eyes when we go to the cinema or watch television.

All kinds of tricks can be played to deceive the eye. Some of the things we see on the screen are clearly impossible—a man might stand face to face with himself and talk to himself; or he may grow into a giant and pick someone up in his hand. But many ordinary scenes that look completely real are also done by camera tricks.

Combining two pictures is one of the most common kinds of special effects. One scene is filmed normally to give a whole picture; this could be a man in close-up holding out his hand. Then another scene is filmed with a black background; this could be the same man seen from a distance so that he looks small. Then the second picture is combined with the first. The black background does not show, and a little figure of the man appears to be standing in his own hand!

With special effects, it is often easier to film in the **studio** instead of going outside. For example, when you see people driving in a car they are often simply sitting in a car which is standing still in the studio, and a moving film of the street is showing on a screen behind them. In the finished film, it looks as if the people are driving along a real street.

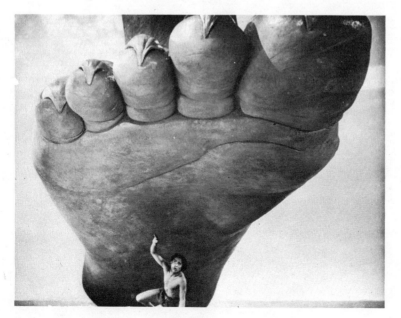

Above: *By special effects, actors perform with cartoon characters in 'Mary Poppins'.*
Right: *The cartoon is drawn, frame by frame over the live film on a transparent sheet. The two.images are combined to make the finished film.*
Left: *The foot of a giant—in fact, a huge model—towers over a boy in 'The Thief of Bagdad'.*

A group is ready to make a record, but it will not be like a normal performance.

First, the music is played without singing. Other parts are then added later.

Next, an orchestra adds more sound to the recorded music.

Finally, all the separate sounds are mixed together by the engineers in the control room to produce a perfect blend of sound.

The master tape in the studio then goes to a cutting room.

There, a master disc is made from the tape.

Moulds for pressing records are made from the master disc.

The voices are added. Many recordings can be made to get a perfect sound.

Records are pressed from the moulds.

Making a Hit Record

Every young musician and singer dreams of making a record. Most of the musicians and singers who do make records are very **talented**, but the recording studio can do a lot to help them sound even better.

Whether you buy a cassette or a record, the music that you hear will have been first recorded on **magnetic tape**. In the main part of the recording studio the **performers** play and sing into microphones. Behind a double glass window is the sound-proof control room, where the engineers and record producer work. The sound from the microphones goes in to a large tape recorder in the control room. The tape may be as much as five centimetres wide and it is possible to record as many as 24 separate sounds on it at once.

The performers hear their music played back over huge speakers. But in the control room is the recording console, which is a magnificent machine covered with a multitude of knobs, switches, dials and coloured lights. The console can completely change the sound that has been recorded—make it harsh, bright, smooth or dull; crisp and clear or distant and echoing. Loud sounds can be made soft and soft sounds made loud, until exactly the right mixture of sound is produced.

If a song or piece of music is not exactly right, the performers do not have to do it all again. Only the parts which are not very good need to be repeated. Then the separate tapes of the best pieces are joined together to give a complete performance. This process is called editing, and it is so well done that the joins in the tape can never be heard. Editing and sound mixing might seem like cheating, but they result in the very best performance on the record.

Right: *the American singer, Elvis Presley, has received 28 golden records. A golden record is awarded after a record has sold a million or more copies. Elvis is the only solo recording star to have had so many golden records.*

87

This schoolgirl has to do her evening's homework at the same time that her favourite ballet programme is on television.

Action Replay

Missing a favourite programme on television because you have to go out or are busy at school or work need no longer upset you. For many years most television programmes have been recorded so they can be shown at any time. Now it is possible to buy a **video** recorder for use in the home. The recorder is plugged into the television set and can record a programme just as a cassette player can record a radio programme. Then, when you have time to sit down, you simply press a button and the machine plays back the programme for you to watch. You can keep the recording and watch the programme again.

It is also possible to plug the video recorder into a small television camera and make your own television film. The recorder keeps the picture taken by the camera and will show it on your television set. This way of making a film is very useful because it can be instantly played back and a scene repeated if anything has gone wrong. When you see a replay on television of a goal just scored, or the winning point at Wimbledon Tennis Championships, you are watching a video recording of

Above: *Later, when she has finished her homework, she can see the ballet programme.*

In the next room the girl's father is watching the ballet programme but he is also recording it on a video recorder so that his daughter does not miss the programme.

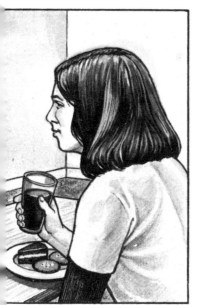

the action instantly played back to show you the exciting moment again.

The video recorder, which will record and play back, works with **magnetic tape**. A television camera produces **electric signals** that a television set changes into a picture. The video recorder simply keeps the signals that come from the camera on magnetic tape, just as a tape recorder does, and will reproduce them whenever the tape is played back.

Several video recorders will only play back programmes which have been recorded all ready for you. The television signals are recorded on a disc or on film. The disc or film is played back in much the same way as a gramophone record or cassette is played. The recorder again plugs into a television set. In video discs, the signals may be recorded in a groove as with a gramophone record. A pick-up, like the needle in a record player, placed in the groove produces the signals, which go to a television set to give the picture and sound.

The disc has to turn very quickly to work, and the pick-up does not in fact touch the groove because the rapid movement of the disc would soon wear it out.

The Sound Machine

Can you imagine a machine that can copy all the instruments of the orchestra, make an explosion or a crash of thunder, chatter away with all the noises of a farmyard, the zoo or even the jungle—and also make strange new sounds that seem to come from the future?

Such a machine is the synthesizer—and it is making a complete change in music. It makes music or noises by **electronics**. Its electric **circuits** produce an electric **signal** that goes to a loudspeaker to be turned into sound. Electronic circuits can now be made very, very small, and the synthesizer produces a wide range of sounds because it contains a great number of circuits. These can be put together in many different ways. Even a small **portable** synthesizer can copy most instruments and produce many sound effects. A large synthesizer can make nearly every sound you can imagine and many you could not imagine. There is only one thing it really cannot do, and that is speak. Human speech is so complicated that machines cannot yet really talk properly. But they will soon.

Until now, copying the sound of instruments on a synthesizer has taken a lot of time and setting the **controls** exactly right has not been easy. However, some synthesizers are now made so that the sounds of a wide range of instruments can be heard just by pressing buttons. The notes are played on a **keyboard**, but what comes out is an electronic sound of a violin, a flute, a trumpet and all the other instruments. The synthesizer is a marvellous development for the **composer**, who can make his own music, and **record** it instantly, without having an **orchestra** to play it. But musicians are less happy about the synthesizer and some fear it may take their place and put them out of work.

In fact, people prefer to see and listen to other people playing music rather than machines, and synthesizers are not often seen in live concerts. However, a lot of music heard on recordings is made with synthesizers, and synthesizer music is also heard on radio and television.

The synthesizer gets its name because it synthesizes (builds up) sounds by putting together basic sounds in many different ways.

Right: *The keyboard player in a rock band gets to work on his synthesizer. By adjusting the controls, the instrument can produce a fantastic range of sounds.*

ANCIENT BUILDINGS

The builders of times gone by created some astonishing structures. No modern monument is as wonderful as the Great Pyramid. Ancient Greek buildings have long been thought so beautiful that they have been copied in public buildings throughout the world.

This temple (below) beside the River Nile in Egypt was cut out of rock about 3,250 years ago. Flooding caused by the building of the Aswan High Dam would have submerged the temple, but engineers have now raised it above the water level.

The Great Pyramid

The Great Pyramid is the only one of the Seven Wonders of the world that is still standing. But it would be more surprising if such a colossal structure were to have disappeared, even though it is nearly 5,000 years old. The pyramid stands 137 metres high (though it has lost its top and was originally nine metres higher) and it measures 230 metres along each side of the base.

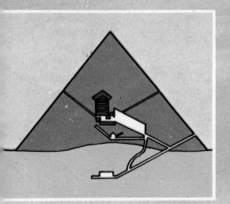

Above: *The interior of the Great Pyramid. The king's burial chamber in the centre has a roof made of nine granite slabs, each weighing 30 tonnes.* **Right:** *The pyramid still standing today, 5,000 years old.*

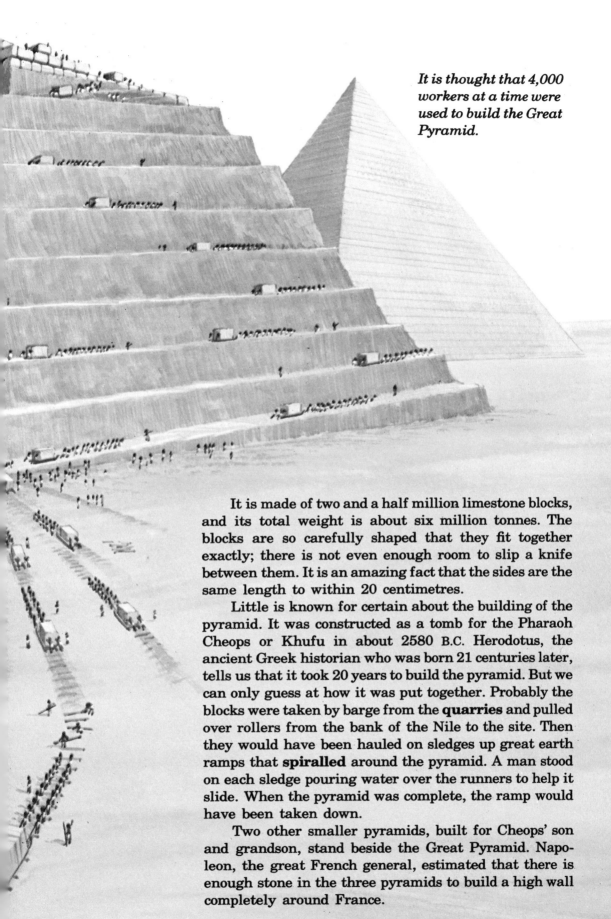

It is thought that 4,000 workers at a time were used to build the Great Pyramid.

It is made of two and a half million limestone blocks, and its total weight is about six million tonnes. The blocks are so carefully shaped that they fit together exactly; there is not even enough room to slip a knife between them. It is an amazing fact that the sides are the same length to within 20 centimetres.

Little is known for certain about the building of the pyramid. It was constructed as a tomb for the Pharaoh Cheops or Khufu in about 2580 B.C. Herodotus, the ancient Greek historian who was born 21 centuries later, tells us that it took 20 years to build the pyramid. But we can only guess at how it was put together. Probably the blocks were taken by barge from the **quarries** and pulled over rollers from the bank of the Nile to the site. Then they would have been hauled on sledges up great earth ramps that **spiralled** around the pyramid. A man stood on each sledge pouring water over the runners to help it slide. When the pyramid was complete, the ramp would have been taken down.

Two other smaller pyramids, built for Cheops' son and grandson, stand beside the Great Pyramid. Napoleon, the great French general, estimated that there is enough stone in the three pyramids to build a high wall completely around France.

95

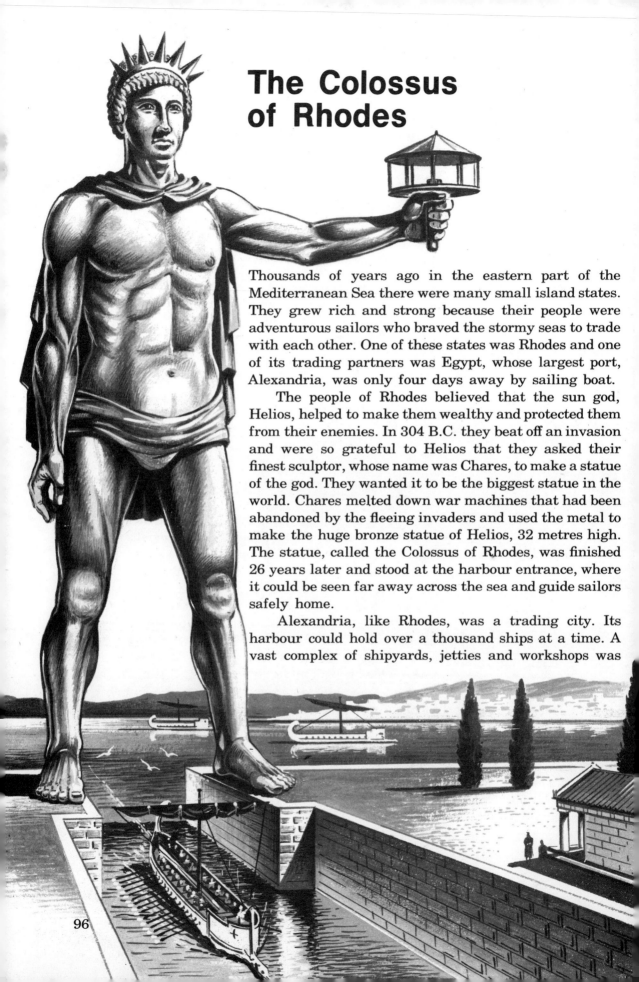

The Colossus of Rhodes

Thousands of years ago in the eastern part of the Mediterranean Sea there were many small island states. They grew rich and strong because their people were adventurous sailors who braved the stormy seas to trade with each other. One of these states was Rhodes and one of its trading partners was Egypt, whose largest port, Alexandria, was only four days away by sailing boat.

The people of Rhodes believed that the sun god, Helios, helped to make them wealthy and protected them from their enemies. In 304 B.C. they beat off an invasion and were so grateful to Helios that they asked their finest sculptor, whose name was Chares, to make a statue of the god. They wanted it to be the biggest statue in the world. Chares melted down war machines that had been abandoned by the fleeing invaders and used the metal to make the huge bronze statue of Helios, 32 metres high. The statue, called the Colossus of Rhodes, was finished 26 years later and stood at the harbour entrance, where it could be seen far away across the sea and guide sailors safely home.

Alexandria, like Rhodes, was a trading city. Its harbour could hold over a thousand ships at a time. A vast complex of shipyards, jetties and workshops was

Lighthouse at Alexandria

Opposite page: *The Colossus of Rhodes as it may have looked in ancient times towering over the entrance to the harbour.*

Left: *The lighthouse at Alexandria, as well as many other devices, had a giant periscope through which ships could be sighted as they appeared on the horizon.*

constructed in the strip of water between the mainland and the island of Pharos just off the coast.

On this island was built a lighthouse about 140 metres high which loomed over the water like a skyscraper. It had hundreds of tiny windows, and from the top a polished stone reflected the sun by day and a **beacon** burned brightly through the night. The lighthouse was built in about 270 B.C. of limestone, marble and granite in three levels like a wedding cake. The bottom layer contained water-driven machinery designed to lift fuel up to the next level. On this middle level horse-drawn wagons hauled wood for the beacon up a spiral ramp. On the top floor, eight columns supported a large stone cup which held the fire.

Both the Colossus of Rhodes and the Lighthouse of Alexandria fell into the sea during earthquakes, and no longer exist. But their names live on in our language—our word colossal comes from a Greek word.

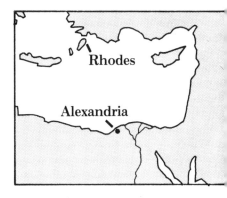

Above: *Rhodes is an island situated off the coast of Turkey. Alexandria lies near the mouth of the Nile.*

Hanging Gardens of Babylon

In ancient times on the banks of the River Euphrates in what is now Iraq was a great city called Babylon. It occupied an exact square on the broad flat plain of the river valley and was surrounded by 96 kilometres of walls 26 metres thick and 46 metres high. The walls were made of clay from the river bed, mixed with tough reeds and made into bricks. One hundred brass gates led into perfectly straight main streets criss-crossing the city. There were many magnificent buildings within the walls of Babylon but the most famous were the extraordinary gardens which appeared to float in the air as if hanging from invisible threads.

The ruler of Babylon, Nebuchadrezzar II, was married to a Persian princess who became homesick for the hills of her own country. To please his wife, Nebuchad-

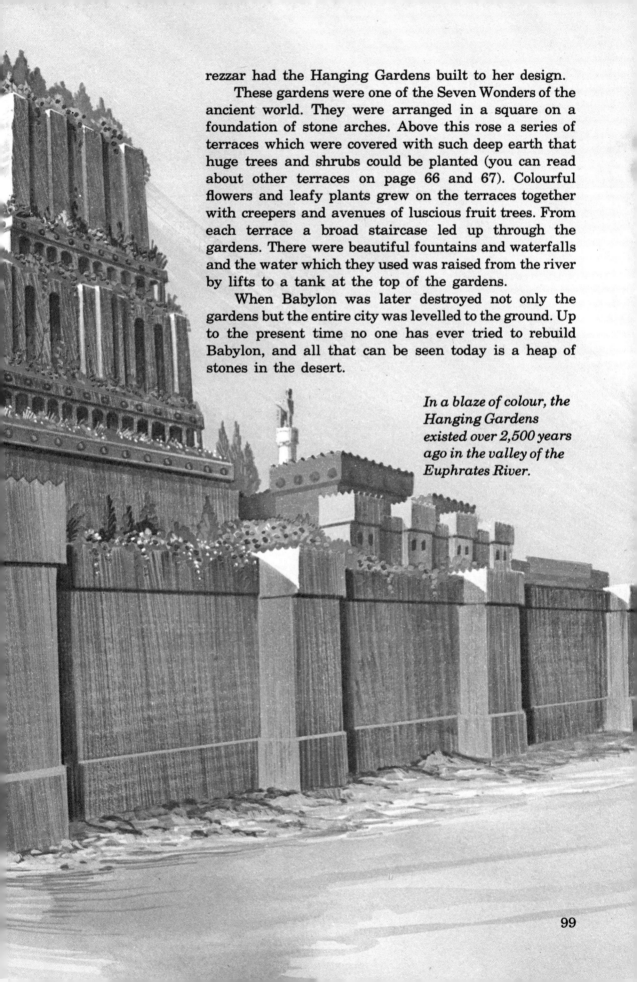

rezzar had the Hanging Gardens built to her design.

These gardens were one of the Seven Wonders of the ancient world. They were arranged in a square on a foundation of stone arches. Above this rose a series of terraces which were covered with such deep earth that huge trees and shrubs could be planted (you can read about other terraces on page 66 and 67). Colourful flowers and leafy plants grew on the terraces together with creepers and avenues of luscious fruit trees. From each terrace a broad staircase led up through the gardens. There were beautiful fountains and waterfalls and the water which they used was raised from the river by lifts to a tank at the top of the gardens.

When Babylon was later destroyed not only the gardens but the entire city was levelled to the ground. Up to the present time no one has ever tried to rebuild Babylon, and all that can be seen today is a heap of stones in the desert.

In a blaze of colour, the Hanging Gardens existed over 2,500 years ago in the valley of the Euphrates River.

The Taj Mahal

The Taj Mahal, at Agra in northern India, is one of the most beautiful buildings in the world. It looks like a gorgeous palace straight from the pages of the **Arabian Nights,** but, in fact, it is a tomb. It was built by the Emperor Shah Jahan for his wife Mumtaz Mahal, who died after giving birth to her 14th child. Shah Jahan did not care how much it would cost. He employed the Indian **architect** Ustad I'sa and searched the world for the finest artists and craftsmen. They began work in 1632 and 22 years later the Taj Mahal was finished.

The Taj Mahal stands on a bank at a bend in the

The Taj Mahal in India looks like a palace, but it is, in fact, a tomb. It took about 20,000 men 22 years to build.

River Jumna, surrounded by high walls with turrets. Its beautiful **minarets** and **domes** of white marble rise elegantly above the high walls. The tomb lies amid gardens with avenues of trees and quiet pools which reflect this wonderful building. Shah Jahan planned to build a similar tomb in black on the opposite side of the River Jumna. But the Shah's son, Aurangzeb, imprisoned his father before the black tomb could be built. From his prison in the fortress at Agra, Shah Jahan would gaze at the Taj Mahal from his cell window. When he died he was buried next to his wife in the Taj Mahal.

The tomb seems to change colour through the day. From a pearly grey at dawn it becomes glistening white at noon and tinged with pink in the evening.

Temple of the Goddess

Most cities in ancient Greece had an acropolis. This was a hill where important temples and public buildings could be found. The most famous one is the Acropolis at Athens. On the slopes of the hill, among the olive trees, were many beautiful buildings and on top of the hill was the most magnificent of all, the Parthenon.

The Parthenon was a temple of the goddess Athena, who protected Athens and from whom the city got its name. Forty-six stone columns supported a marvellous carved stone picture which ran around the top of the building. The stone picture showed many scenes from the history of Athens and stories about the gods. When they were first made, these stone carvings would have been painted in brilliant colours. The building was designed by Iktinos and Callicrates and the carvings made by Phidias between 447 and 432 B.C. Phidias also made a huge statue of Athena nearby. This stood over nine metres high and was made of bronze, covered with gold and studded with thousands of jewels. The tip of her

Below: *The Acropolis as it looked in ancient times. Nearly all the buildings are now in ruins* (**pictured above**), *though enough remains to give a good idea of what they originally looked like.*

102

spear could be seen glistening in the sun by Athenian sailors in ships out at sea.

Among the other temples on the Acropolis was the Erectheum, which was also dedicated to Athena. Instead of columns, the porch of this temple had caryatids. Caryatids were pillars carved in the shapes of goddesses. They seem to carry the roof on their heads. Animals were sacrificed to Athena in the temples and rich offerings of treasure were stored there. The Acropolis was also the centre for festivals and celebrations.

Very little of this magnificence now remains. Athens has been attacked and destroyed by its enemies many times. The statue of Athena has completely disappeared. The great buildings of the Acropolis are in ruins and parts of them have been taken to museums all over the world.

Biggest object in the world

One single structure built by man is so large that it can possibly be seen from a space capsule. This is the Great Wall of China. It has the biggest volume of anything made by man, being about 100 times as big as the Great Pyramid. The Great Wall extends across northern China, running across mountains and valleys without a break.

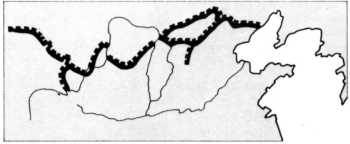

When China's first emperor, Shih Huang Ti, decided to link his frontier forts he built the Great Wall of China. The Wall winds across mountains and valleys for about 4,000 kilometres from the Gulf of Pohai to Kansu. It is long enough to stretch nearly three and a half times down the length of Great Britain.

It is up to ten metres high and ten metres thick, and is about 4,000 kilometres long.

The Great Wall was completed in the third century B.C. by the emperor Shih Huang Ti. It could have taken 300,000 men ten years to build the Great Wall, which formed the northern frontier of the Chinese Empire. It was abandoned in the sixth century A.D. when China's frontier changed. However, the Ming emperors later restored the Great Wall to keep the **Mongols** from invading China. They ruled from 1368 to 1644, after which the Wall again fell into disrepair. Recently sections of it have been rebuilt.

The Wall is faced with stone and brick, but filled with earth and rubble. Watch towers are placed short distances apart, and at greater intervals come gateways and **fortresses**. The Wall was built to prevent invaders entering China, and at weak points several extra walls were built to strengthen defences. However, the Great Wall also served as a roadway, for carriages could be driven along the top. In mountainous regions it would certainly have been the best route to take.

The Colosseum

The people who lived long ago had no cinema or television to entertain them, instead they would go to the theatre or **arenas** where the great games were held. The Greeks and the Romans built many big open-air theatres and stadiums, but none were as magnificent as the Colosseum in Rome.

It was a vast oval building, 188 metres across. Around the central arena rose level upon level of marble seats; when a great show was held at the Colosseum, as many as 50,000 people would crowd into it. A canvas sunshade supported by a circle of poles protected the crowd from the hot sun. The Colosseum was begun in about 70 A.D. and it took ten years to build. In many ways, it was like a modern stadium. There were 80 entrances around the outside wall and all the seats were numbered. Ivory tickets were issued for the shows and

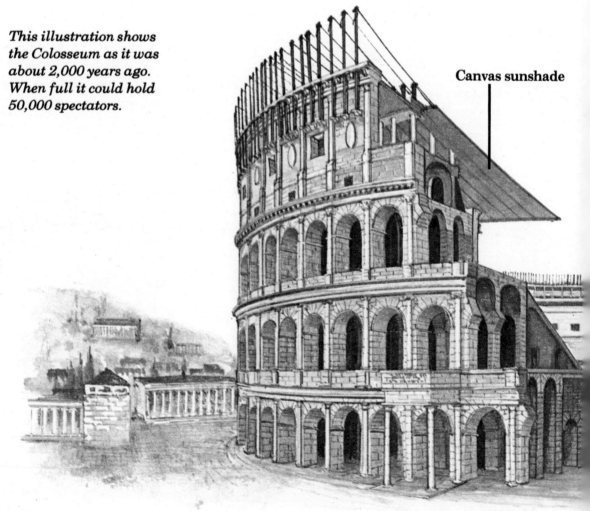

This illustration shows the Colosseum as it was about 2,000 years ago. When full it could hold 50,000 spectators.

Canvas sunshade

each was marked with the number of the entrance, row and seat so that everyone could find their place quickly and easily. And, just like today, the most expensive seats were at the front.

The Colosseum was an amphitheatre—this means 'a round theatre', as the arena was surrounded by the audience on all sides. It was the best equipped of all Roman amphitheatres. At first, athletics contests and chariot races were held there. It was even possible to flood the arena with water and have shows with boats. There were also shows with wild animals from the distant parts of the Roman Empire—such as lions, leopards, bulls and elephants. As time went on, the shows at the Colosseum became cruel and bloodthirsty. Gladiators—who were usually slaves or prisoners—were made to fight with each other to the death or to fight the animals. Many thousands of people and animals were brutally killed during these events, which often lasted for months at a time. The floor was spread with sand to soak up the blood. To protect the crowd, and to stop the gladiators or the animals escaping, a moat and high wall surrounded the arena.

Above: *The Colosseum still stands in Rome, but it is now in ruins. The floor of the arena has gone, but beneath can be seen the walls of the cages and cells where the animals and prisoners were held.*

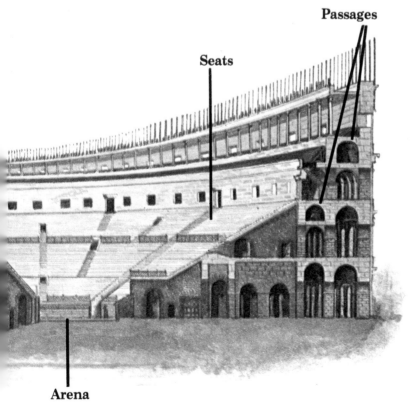

Passages

Seats

Arena

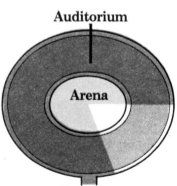

Auditorium

Arena

Entrance

Above: *A diagram showing the shape of the complete Colosseum. The grey area shows the piece of the stadium that has been left out of the illustration.*

Pyramid City

Hidden in the jungle of the Khmer Republic (formerly Cambodia) lies one of the most amazing ancient cities of the world. It is called Angkor Thom, and it was founded in the ninth century by the Khmer kings, who followed the **Hindu religion**. They constructed the city to express their religious ideas of the Universe. From each gate in the outer walls, avenues lined with carved stone figures each holding a sacred **cobra** lead up to a great high temple in the centre of the city.

The temple was built like a mountain and covered with detailed carvings showing scenes from Khmer history and Hindu legends. The temple towered over the pyramid-shaped city just as the people's gods ruled the Universe. Yet the gods failed the city. In 1431 Siamese invaders sacked Angkor Thom and the city was abandoned as the Khmer Empire fell. Gradually the jungle

Above: *The central temple of Angkor Wat, the great temple complex of the Khmer kings. The temple complex is so big that Hindu pilgrims who wanted to go round the temple had to walk over 20 kilometres.*
Right: *A battle scene carved into a wall at Angkor Wat.*

grew again and the city vanished.

Just to the south lay a huge temple named Angkor Wat. It was built by King Suryavarman II in the twelfth century. Its outer wall, nearly a kilometre long, is adorned with carvings depicting the king's life and Hindu legends. The buildings of the temple rise to a high central point, giving it the shape of a pyramid similar to that of the nearby city.

Monks remained in Angkor Wat after the city fell, and it became a centre for **pilgrims** to visit. French **archaeologists** came there in about 1860 and realized that a huge city lay lost in the jungle nearby.

Left: *The road which leads to Angkor Wat is a wide stone causeway, crossing a moat 190 metres wide.* **Below:** *On each side of the causeway is a row of great statues of Khmer giants holding a huge serpent.*

Lost City

A small band of Spanish adventurers, less than 200 men, destroyed the ancient civilization of the Inca people of Peru in the 1500s. The Inca people thought their king was a Sun god and obeyed him in everything. By capturing the king the Spaniards easily overran his empire. But there was one city they missed—the lost city of the Incas.

In 1911 an American explorer named Hiram Bingham rediscovered the city high in the Andes Mountains. It lay on a mountain top more than 2,000 metres high, hidden in jungle. Beneath the thick **vegetation** were the ruins of a marvellous city. As the site was cleared, the remains of temples, palaces and towers came to light.

The buildings, reached by staircases that ran everywhere, were surrounded by terraced gardens; fountains played, and on all sides there was a superb view of the mountains. In the city was a special sundial that helped the Incas to make an accurate calendar. This was an important find, for the Spaniards had destroyed the sundials elsewhere.

Machu Picchu, as the city is called, also has a mystery. Many skeletons were found when the city was **excavated**, but nearly all of them were female. Possibly they were priestesses who had fled to Machu Picchu to escape the attack on Cuzco, the Inca capital, 80 kilometres away.

Buildings in the Sky

In a remote river valley in northern Greece stands a group of strange **pinnacles** of rock. They rise high into the air from the valley side, looking out over the river below like guards on watch. And built on the tops of several of the rocks are old **monasteries**. A few monks and nuns live in the monasteries, welcoming visitors with a glass of water and a few grapes as refreshment after their long climb.

It is well worth the effort, for the walls and ceilings of the churches inside the monasteries are decorated with beautiful paintings. And it is pleasant to spend a few moments as the monks and nuns often do, quietly

Opposite page: *One of the ancient monasteries perched high on a pinnacle of rock at Meteora which is in a remote part of central Greece.* **Far right:** *Visitors were once hauled up to the monasteries in a net.*

GREECE

Meteora

looking at the magnificent scenery and thinking deep thoughts. There is work to be done, too, for all supplies are hauled up in a net from the ground below. A **windlass** turned by the monks themselves pulls in the rope attached to the net.

This strange place is called Meteora, a Greek word meaning 'things of the air'. It is a good name for these buildings in the sky. The first monastery was built in about 1350 by monks who wanted to escape from robbers in the valley and to find a place to lead their peaceful lives. Eagles and vultures fly around, and a **legend** has it that the first monk was carried up by an eagle.

Just as unbelievable is the way the monasteries are built, their walls rising from ledges on steep rock faces. The Meteora monasteries remained totally cut off from the world until about 50 years ago, when steps were made in the rocks to allow easy access. Before then, any visitor had to be hauled up in a net just as supplies were. Some of the monasteries are now deserted, for few people want to take up the life of a monk or nun nowadays. But others have been restored to their former glory.

St Paul's Cathedral

The Great Fire of London in 1666 burned down most of the city, but it also did some good. It finally removed the **plague** from London, which had killed thousands during the previous year. It also destroyed old St Paul's Cathedral, allowing Sir Christopher Wren to build the magnificent domed cathedral that now stands out on London's skyline. The cathedral was started in 1675 and completed in 1710.

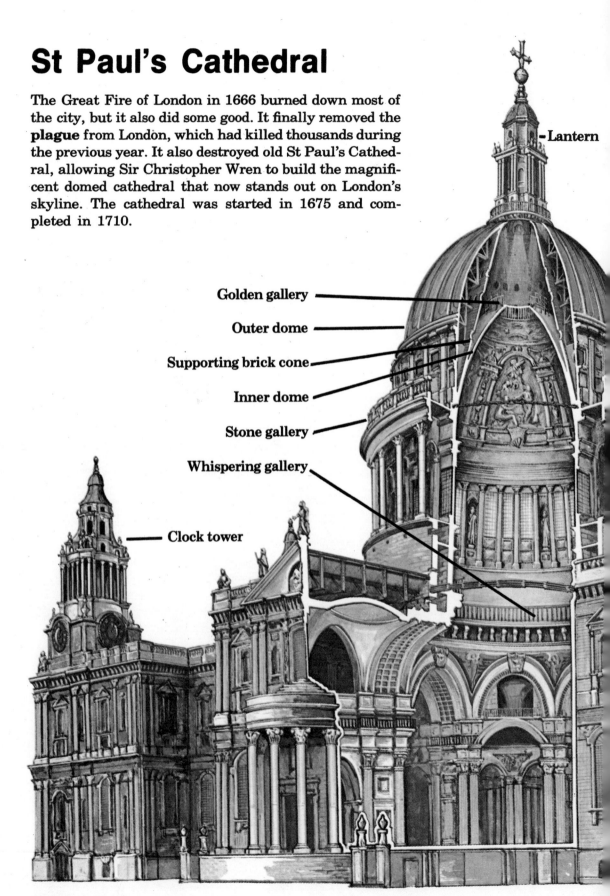

Lantern

Golden gallery

Outer dome

Supporting brick cone

Inner dome

Stone gallery

Whispering gallery

Clock tower

It has the largest dome of any church, except for St Peter's Basilica in Rome. There are, in fact, two domes —an inner dome of brick and an outer dome of timber covered with lead. In between the two domes is a stairway that leads to the Golden Gallery at the top of the dome. It is even possible to climb to the ball on the top of the lantern above the dome, though 627 steps must be climbed from the ground to get there. Also between the two domes is a huge cone of brick. The lantern, which is very heavy, rests on this cone and not on the dome.

At the base of the outer dome is the Stone Gallery, from which a good view of London can be had without climbing all the way to the top of the dome. But the most interesting gallery is the Whispering Gallery which is inside at the base of the inner dome. It gets its unusual name because a whisper made on one side of the gallery can be clearly heard at the other side, 33 metres away. The reason is that the circular shape of the dome reflects the sound from one side to the other.

The cathedral was miraculously saved from harm during the Second World War. All the surrounding buildings were destroyed, but the cathedral was not badly hit. However, a small bomb blew out most of the beautiful stained glass.

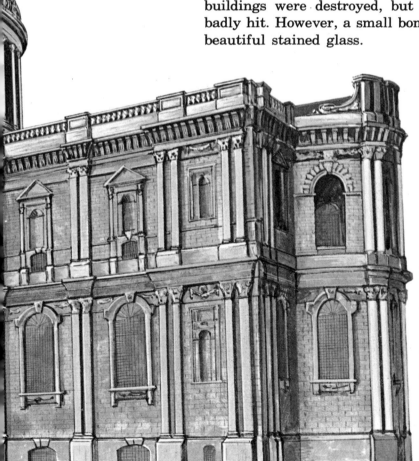

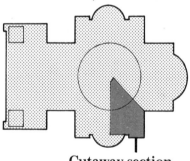

Cutaway section

Above: *This plan diagram shows the section that has been taken out of the illustration so that the inside of the cathedral can be seen.*

City of Mud

For thousands of years, ever since the most ancient times, people have built houses from mud. In Jericho, the oldest city in the world, the remains of mud houses have been found that are at least 7,000 years old. Mud walls are not made by simply piling handfuls of mud on top of each other.

A building made like this would crack as it dried and come down easily. Instead, mud bricks are made by mixing wet clay with straw or grass and drying them in the sun. The straw or grass holds the clay together. The walls are built by laying the bricks in rows and filling in the gaps with mud.

People can make their own houses in this way, and they are simple to mend when necessary. The mud walls are fairly strong, and they keep out the weather. In

Above: *Part of the huge mud wall surrounding the city.*

Right: *The ancient mud city of Kano. All these buildings are made of clay and earth, packed together and strong enough to have lasted for hundreds of years.*
Below: *Kano is situated in the north of Nigeria in West Africa.*

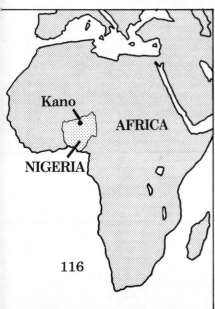

116

places that are warm and dry, mud is a good building material and mud dwellings are still found in places at the edges of deserts.

At Kano, in northern Nigeria, on the edge of the Sahara Desert, there is an ancient city of mud. Kano was once the **capital** of the ancient kingdom of the Hausa people. It was built about 900 years ago, and the old city is still there as part of modern Kano. The old city contains thousands of square, flat-roofed mud houses, and is surrounded by a huge mud wall, 12 metres wide at the base and nine to 15 metres high.

Inside the city are large pools and pits where the mud is dug out to make the houses. Its size is enormous—the wall is 20 kilometres long—for ancient Kano was an important city. Caravans (long lines of camels carrying supplies) came from across the desert to trade goods in Kano's old market, at one time using shells, instead of coins, as money.

117

MODERN BUILDINGS

Every city has something that makes it different from other cities. A few have ancient monuments that make them famous throughout the world—such as the Parthenon at Athens and the Colosseum in Rome. Most cities have modern buildings or structures that serve as a symbol of the city. Paris has the Eiffel Tower, New York the Statue of Liberty, Sydney its strange new Opera House. San Francisco has a wonderful modern pyramid called the Transamerica Building which is shown below.

The Rocket Building

Many cities have a tower as a **symbol**. London has the old Tower of London, once a fortress, and the new Post Office Tower, a **communications centre**. Paris has a tower built purely as a symbol—the Eiffel Tower, built in 1889 for a great **exhibition**. In modern times, uses have been found for these towers. As well as providing a view over the city for tourists, they carry a mast to send

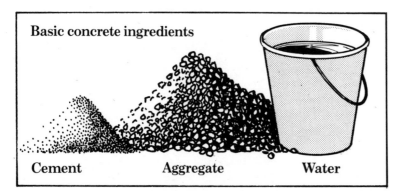

Basic concrete ingredients

Cement   Aggregate   Water

Left: The Tower is made of concrete which is nothing more than a mixture of cement, stone, sand and water. By strengthening it with steel bars, tall structures can be built. **Opposite page and below:** *The rocket-like CN Tower dominates the city of Toronto, Canada. The Tower is the tallest self-supporting structure in the world.*

television and radio programmes to the people of the city.

Now a new tower has joined the famous towers of the world's cities and it will become a world-famous landmark. This is the CN Tower in Toronto, Canada, which opened in 1976. Standing like a rocket among Toronto's skyscrapers, it towers 553 metres into the air. At the bottom of the Tower is a lake and specially built **terraces** for the people of the city.

A bridge leads visitors to the Tower's entrance, and then a lift whisks them up to the Sky Pod, 350 metres above. A wall of the lift is made of glass, so that visitors can see the city dropping away below during their one-minute ride. The Sky Pod is large and round and contains a 400-seat **revolving** restaurant. There are observation platforms both at this level and at another level 100 metres higher, and on a clear day visitors can see more than 100 kilometres in all directions.

The CN Tower is not just a place for viewing and eating, spectacular though it may be. It was built by Canadian National Railways as a communications centre, and it also has a television and radio mast.

The Tower is the highest self-supporting building in the world, and its shape, which looks like something from the future, is made possible by building in **pre-stressed concrete**, a material that combines the different strengths of concrete and steel so that almost any shaped building can be constructed.

Reaching for the Sky

If a city really wants to look modern, then it has to have some skyscrapers. Although these towering buildings have been with us for over a hundred years, skyscrapers still seem to mean progress to people. Such buildings certainly do present an impressive appearance as they reach into the sky. Some are so tall that they sometimes disappear into the clouds.

For a tourist, the view from the top of a skyscraper is always superb, even though it may be so windy that the eyes water all the time. And the ride up and down in a high-speed lift can be exciting. But people who have to work in skyscrapers may not be so happy.

Such tall buildings mean that a great number of people must live or work closely together and this can mean problems in city transport. Also, a row of skyscrapers along each side of a street turns it into a dark canyon where the sun never shines. For these reasons skyscrapers are seldom to be seen huddling close together in cities. Rather they stand aloof and proud as other buildings cluster around their feet.

No skyscraper could be built until a safe lift had been invented. This was done by an American engineer named Elisha Otis in 1853. He found a way of stopping a lift from falling if the cable should break. The first skyscrapers were built soon after this invention was made, although today we think of them as just high buildings. Buildings in New York rose to 40 metres in height by 1870.

Then the use of steel frameworks to hold buildings together meant skyscrapers could be built to reach dizzy heights. The framework held the load of the floors and roofs and also the walls, so that the walls no longer had to be built thick and strong to hold up the buildings. There was no need for deep **foundations**, but underlying rock was necessary to support the weight of the skyscraper. In cities that are built on softer materials, such as London, there are no very high skyscrapers because it would not be safe to build them.

Skyscrapers began to shoot into the air in American cities, particularly in New York. The Empire State Building, 381 metres high, was the world's tallest inhabited building for a long time. This world record has now passed to the Sears Tower in Chicago, which is 553 metres high and also has the fastest passenger lift which can travel at a speed of 33 kilometres an hour. Skyscrapers may reach heights of 600 metres by the year 2000.

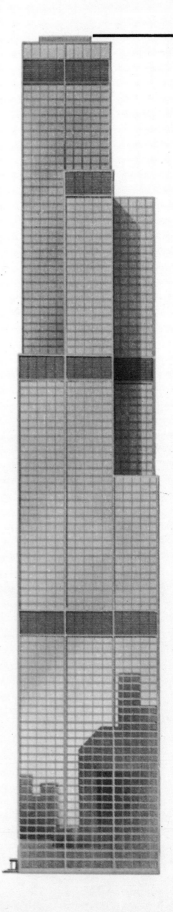

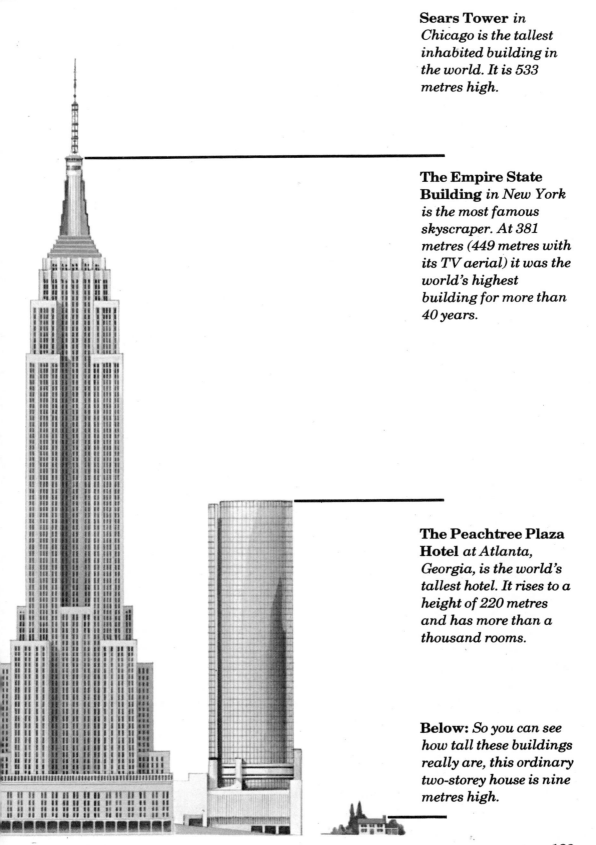

Sears Tower *in Chicago is the tallest inhabited building in the world. It is 533 metres high.*

The Empire State Building *in New York is the most famous skyscraper. At 381 metres (449 metres with its TV aerial) it was the world's highest building for more than 40 years.*

The Peachtree Plaza Hotel *at Atlanta, Georgia, is the world's tallest hotel. It rises to a height of 220 metres and has more than a thousand rooms.*

Below: *So you can see how tall these buildings really are, this ordinary two-storey house is nine metres high.*

123

Louisiana Superdome

Cities have monuments of all kinds—towers, great statues, skyscrapers, magnificent opera houses. When the people of the state of Louisiana in the United States thought about what kind of monument they would like, they voted for an indoor **stadium**. They did not want just any stadium, but one as large as the Colosseum in Rome. (You can read about the Colosseum on pages 106 and 107.) And it had to have a roof so that it could be used for all kinds of entertainment at all times of year. In 1974 they finished building the Louisiana Superdome, the world's largest indoor stadium topped with the world's largest dome, 82 metres high and 210 metres across. It rises above the famous old streets of New Orleans, Louisiana's biggest city.

The Superdome is not only a sports stadium, although it can seat a crowd of 80,000 beneath the dome to watch **American football**. The size of the **arena** and the seating can be changed so that people can watch all kinds of sports, but it can also be changed to present concerts, contests, parades, circuses, **conventions** and exhibitions. For a giant convention, nearly 100,000 people can be seated in the Superdome!

In most stadiums you have to buy an expensive seat to be near the front and see and hear well—but not in the Supedrome. Suspended from the centre of the dome are six huge colour television screens giving close-up views

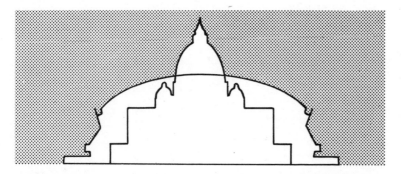

of the action. Each screen is nearly a thousand times larger in area than a home television screen. Wherever you sit in the Superdome, you will get a good view and you will be able to hear well, as there are speakers for sound all around the vast stadium. Instant replay on the television screens gives a second look at exciting moments, and there is no need to leave when the game or show is over, for the television presentation continues with interviews and replays.

Above: *The Louisiana Superdome rises into the New Orleans skyline like a huge flying saucer.*
Left: *The size of the Superdome compared with St. Peter's Basilica in Rome.*

Right: *The interior of the world's largest enclosed stadium. The Superdome is filled to capacity as the audience watch an impressive parade.*

124

Instant City

Brazil is the fifth largest country in the world, but almost all of its land is covered in thick forest and jungle. To make use of this land, President Kubitschek of Brazil decided in 1957 that a new **capital** city called Brasilia should be built far inland. The city was to be ready in three years, and would then replace the previous capital, Rio de Janeiro.

Work started immediately. As there were no proper roads to the **site**, the first materials had to be flown in by air while the roads and railways were being built to span the 1000 kilometres from the coast to the central highlands. At enormous cost the proud new capital rose from the jungle. In 1960 it was ready. The government of Brazil moved to Brasilia and began the hard but vital task of developing the rest of Brazil.

Brasilia is a city of the future. The shapes of the buildings are completely different from other modern buildings in other capital cities. But Brasilia is also planned to make life safe and happy for its half-a-million people. It is shaped like a bow and arrow. In the bow-shaped section are the **residential** areas, complete with parks as well as houses and flats.

The roads are designed to separate traffic from people, to avoid accidents. The arrow-shaped section is made up of a long avenue. At its tip are the government buildings, and along the **shaft** are hotels, sports and circus areas, shops and bus and railway stations. Around most of the city is a huge lake.

Left: *The cathedral at Brasilia at night. It is shaped like the crown of thorns.*
Above: *The interior of the cathedral.*
Below: *The Brasilia government buildings.*

Welcome to America

The United States gained its **independence** from Britain in 1776. To mark the hundredth **anniversary** of this event, France decided to give the United States a statue. It was to be placed at the entrance of New York harbour, where it would welcome new Americans.

The French **sculptor**, Frédéric-Auguste Bartholdi, started work in 1874 and built several models first. Each model was larger than the one before, and eventually the

Right: *Around the torch of the statue is a balcony. A ladder inside the right arm leads up to it, but this is not now open to the public.*
Opposite page: *The Statue of Liberty welcomes people who arrive at New York by ship. Nearly a million people visit the statue every year.*

huge statue was ready for delivery to the United States.

In 1885, it was shipped in 300 huge copper pieces to New York and put together over a vast **framework** made by Gustave Eiffel, the man who built the Eiffel Tower in Paris. The following year it was named the Statue of Liberty.

The statue is of a woman holding a torch aloft in her right hand as a welcoming **beacon**. In her left hand is a book, which stands for the **Declaration of Independence**, and at her feet are some broken **shackles**, to show that America is free.

The whole statue is 45 metres high and weighs 225 tonnes. It stands on a huge **pedestal** containing a museum. A lift takes visitors up through the pedestal to the base of the statue, and then inside the statue a circular staircase of 168 steps leads to the crown on the head. There, visitors can look out through windows in the crown over the skyscrapers of New York, and if the visitors turn around they can see over the harbour to the great Verrazano Narrows Bridge (you can read about this bridge on pages 58 and 59).

The Building that Sails

When many people think of Sydney in Australia, they probably still think of the great arch bridge that **spans** the harbour there. However, nearby there is a far more wonderful sight to be found. This is the Sydney Opera House, one of the most beautiful modern buildings in the world.

In the 1950s the city decided it needed a proper centre for its **orchestra** and asked for **designs** for an

Opposite page: *The beautiful white shells of the Opera House at Sydney, Australia. They look like the sails of a yacht sailing in the harbour. The building cost a hundred million Australian dollars.*
Right: *The interior of the Opera House.*

opera house. The winning design was made by the Danish **architect** Joern Otzun. The opera house was to be built at Bennelong Point, a tongue of land sticking out into the waters of the harbour.

The harbour is often dotted with boats, and Otzun decided to make the opera house look like a beautiful great white yacht surrounded by the blue-green waters of the harbour. His design was for a building made of huge shells of concrete covered with silvery tiles, rearing into the air like billowing white sails. The building of the opera house was begun in 1959, but no one knew exactly how to make the great concrete shells. Ways of building the opera house were at last found and it eventually opened in 1973.

The roof is made of 2,414 **segments** of concrete glued together with epoxy resin (you can read about glues on pages 156 and 157). The concrete was then covered with a million tiles. Each segment weighs between 5 and 15 tonnes, and the whole roof weighs over 20,000 tonnes. Inside the opera house is a concert hall, a large theatre for opera and ballet, a small theatre for plays, a cinema, and rehearsal and recording studios.

No Life Can Survive

No place can be more unfriendly than the South Pole. Covered in complete darkness for half the year, tormented by fierce winds and shivering in temperatures that drop as low as —80·C, nothing can live there. Not even **bacteria** live at the South Pole. But important **scientific research** needs to be done at the Pole, and so in 1956 a party of American scientists flew in to build a base in the snow and ice there. Only two people had been there before them—the Norwegian explorer Roald Amundsen, who discovered the Pole in 1911, and the British explorer Robert Scott, who was just beaten by Amundsen and who died on the journey back.

The base was called the Amundsen-Scott South Pole Station, and it soon began to disappear under the snow. The Antarctic ice sheet has been building up for thousands of years as more and more snow falls and is compressed into ice. By 1967 the base was six metres

Opposite page: *The snow-covered dome of the new base at the South Pole.*
Right: *Beneath the unheated dome are working and living quarters for the people on the base.*

under the snow and a new station had to be built. The new station, finished in 1975, is on the surface of the snow and ice and the scientists can work in comfort. They need to be well treated, for the station is cut off from the outside world from February to October, when the six-month night falls.

The main part of the station is a large **dome** 50 metres across. Beneath the dome are three buildings containing a **communications centre**, a store, a library and recreation room, laboratories, living quarters for 23 people, a kitchen and dining hall, a post office, and a meeting hall. Outside the dome are long buildings with arched roofs containing diesel-electric **generators** to provide heat and power, garages for the vehicles, and a gymnasium, as well as high towers for making **scientific observations**. The dome, outside buildings and towers are linked by covered passages. Alongside is the air strip for aircraft to take-off and land.

Above: *All around the base is the great Antarctic ice sheet.*

132

Right: *Visitors are welcomed to the world's loneliest place.*

FROM HERE TO THERE

People have always wanted to travel and see the world. Now, we can do just that at a glance—from the window of a spacecraft! Because we are always looking for faster ways to travel and always searching into the unknown, an amazing array of vehicles has been invented.

Some are beautiful, such as the supersonic airliner Concorde, in the photograph below. Some are exciting, such as the rocket-powered car and the train that hovers on air. Some are strange, such as the buggy that can trundle about on the Moon.

The Jet Engine

The first aircraft, *Flyer I*, built by the Wright brothers in 1903, flew over the ground at eleven kilometres an hour. In fact, it was flying into the wind and so its air speed was somewhat greater. By the beginning of World War II in 1939, air speeds had risen to about 700 kilometres an hour. A faster aircraft would have given any of the fighting countries a great advantage in the war. However, **propeller-driven** planes could not go much faster than 700 kilometres an hour because the propellers would break up if speeds were greater. A new kind of aircraft engine was needed.

Right: *A compressor draws air into the combustion chamber, where it is heated and expands rapidly. As it leaves, the air drives a turbine, which powers the compressor. The jet of air produced thrusts the engine forward.*

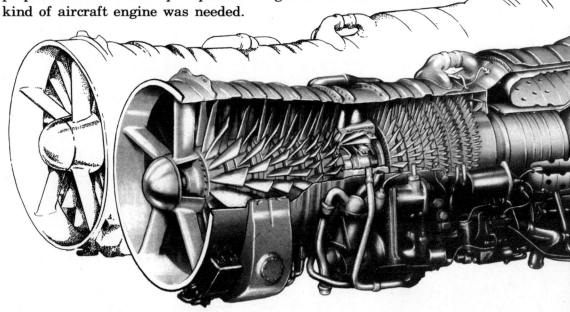

Powered aircraft could fly through the air by pushing air backwards. Spinning propellers act like fans to force air backwards, and the aircraft moves forwards as a result. Higher speeds could only be obtained by making an engine that creates a jet of high speed air. The jet engine was developed during World War II. Jet aircraft flew faster and faster and in 1947 the sound barrier was broken.

Now jet fighters can travel at three times the speed of sound and reach speeds of more than 3000 kilometres an hour. The jet engine has made cheap and fast flight possible, and people are now able to travel wherever they want to go, anywhere in the world, in a matter of hours. **Supersonic airliners** travel at twice the speed of sound —sometimes keeping ahead of the sun as it moves through the sky.

Above: *A jet engine works like a balloon that is blown up and let go with the neck open. Air rushes out of the*

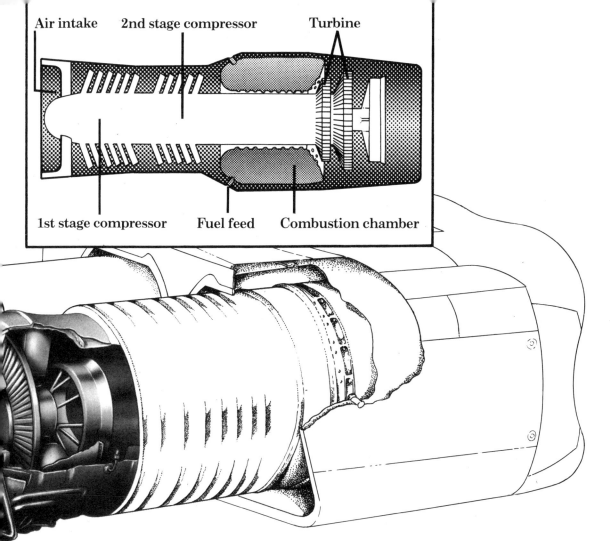

Air intake   2nd stage compressor   Turbine

1st stage compressor   Fuel feed   Combustion chamber

Above: *The inside of the Concorde jet engine.*

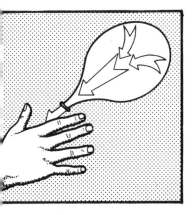

neck, thrusting it forward, just like the jet of air produced by a jet engine moving forward.

The jet engine works by forcing air into a small **combustion** chamber with a spinning **turbine**, and then heating it rapidly in a flame of burning paraffin. The air expands with the heat, and rushes from the engine in a high-speed jet. As it leaves, it spins another turbine which is connected to the first turbine and moves it.

The idea of moving objects by jets of high-speed air has been known for hundreds of years. In the first century A.D. the Greek **engineer**, Hero, built a famous engine in which jets of steam made a ball go round. The ball was hollow and contained some water, and two bent tubes were fixed to the ball. As the ball was heated, the water inside boiled and turned into steam. The steam rushed out from the tubes making the ball go round in the opposite way to where the jets of steam were rushing out. Hero's engine was never put to actual use and was thought of as a toy. The jet engine was invented by the British engineer Sir Frank Whittle, who **patented** the idea in 1930. He built the first test engine in 1937, but he was beaten into the air by the Germans, who first used a jet engine to power an aircraft in 1939.

137

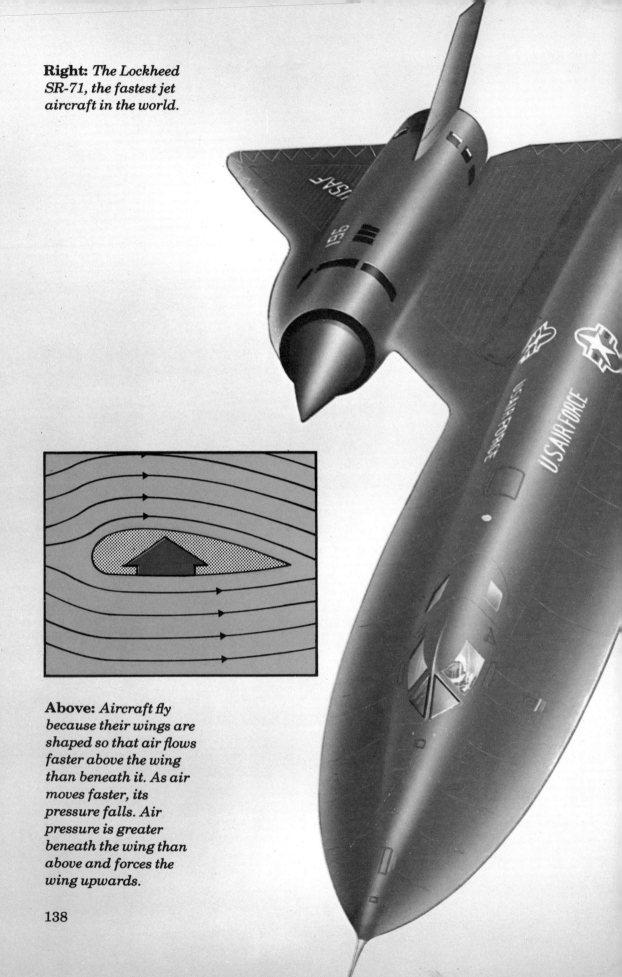

Right: *The Lockheed SR-71, the fastest jet aircraft in the world.*

Above: *Aircraft fly because their wings are shaped so that air flows faster above the wing than beneath it. As air moves faster, its pressure falls. Air pressure is greater beneath the wing than above and forces the wing upwards.*

Faster than Time

The very fastest aircraft can now travel so quickly that they can get to places before they set off! In fact they do not actually travel faster than time but only seem to do so. The fastest aircraft can cross the Atlantic Ocean in two hours. If it leaves London at 4 o'clock it will get to New York when it is 6 o'clock in London. But as New York is five hours behind London, it will only be 1 o'clock there! On its journey, the aircraft overtakes the Sun, and the **crew** add three hours to their day. However, they lose this extra time on making the return journey. If they leave New York at 1 o'clock, they will arrive in London when it is 3 o'clock in New York but 8 o'clock in London!

Passengers in **supersonic airliners** will also seem to travel faster than time when they travel from east to west. The people who travel at the highest speeds however, are the crews of military aircraft. The fastest jet aircraft in the world is an American plane, the Lockheed SR-71, which can reach a speed of about 3,500 kilometres an hour or more than three times the speed of sound. It can keep going like this for an hour and a half, so it can travel nearly 5,000 kilometres. Although it travels so fast, the SR-71 was not built as a fighter aircraft. It flies at a very great height—30,000 metres—and is used to take photographs of the ground below to find out if any country is preparing for war. It has to be fast to escape intercepting aircraft and missiles.

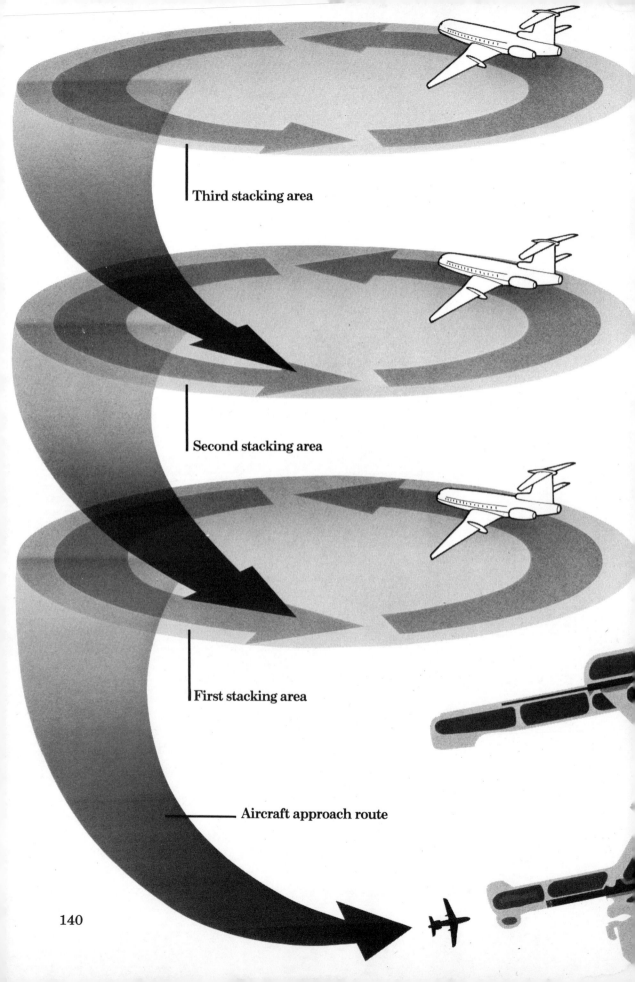

Third stacking area

Second stacking area

First stacking area

Aircraft approach route

Safety in the Skies

Modern airliners travel so fast that **collisions** are very likely to happen if their movements are not well planned, especially at airports. In midflight, high above the clouds, a pilot can see a long way ahead and can easily take avoiding action if another aircraft should come near. In fact, all air routes are planned so that this is very unlikely to happen. But at airports several aircraft may occupy the same air space at the same time. Therefore air traffic controllers direct all aircraft movement to minimize risks of collision.

On taking off, only one airliner may leave at once, and it must be well up and away before the next one leaves. Landing is more of a problem because several aircraft may arrive at once. Also there may be cloud to block the pilot's view or it may be dark. But with instruments and radar (you can read about radar on pages 192 and 193), each pilot knows where he is, and the air traffic controllers at the airport can keep track of all the aircraft. The controllers direct them by radio to form an orderly queue in the sky. On approaching the airport, the pilot enters a **glide path** by following **signals** sent out by automatic radio beacons. The glide path leads the airliner down to the runway and it lands safely.

Many modern aircraft have automatic landing systems that take over from the pilot on the final approach, making it safe to land in fog. **Computer systems** are being developed to take over all air traffic control.

Above: *Inside the control tower at a major international airport. Chicago International, one of the world's busiest airports, in one year handled nearly 700,000 aircraft and 38 million passengers. The air traffic controller has a very responsible job as he has to instruct the aircraft's pilot on what action to take.*

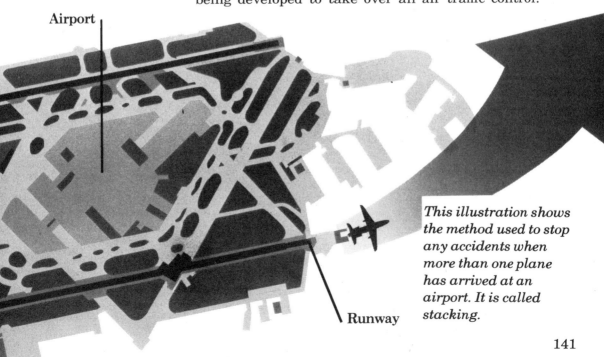

Airport

Runway

This illustration shows the method used to stop any accidents when more than one plane has arrived at an airport. It is called stacking.

Car built for the Moon

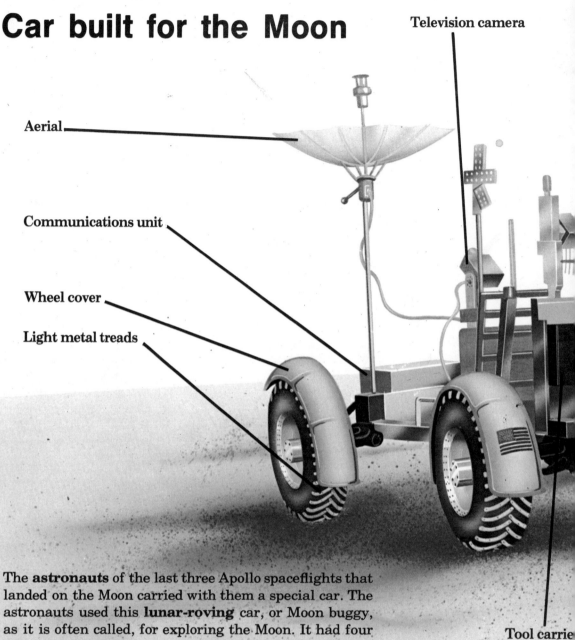

Television camera

Aerial

Communications unit

Wheel cover

Light metal treads

Tool carrie

The **astronauts** of the last three Apollo spaceflights that landed on the Moon carried with them a special car. The astronauts used this **lunar-roving** car, or Moon buggy, as it is often called, for exploring the Moon. It had four wheels and two seats, but was otherwise no ordinary car. Its wheels were made of a flexible net of interwoven wire covered with light metal **treads**. They were large enough to drive over obstacles 30 centimetres high and cross cracks in the ground 70 centimetres wide. Each wheel was driven by its own electric motor powered by batteries. It could travel at up to 18 kilometres an hour.

The buggy could climb slopes as steep as 25 degrees, and it could travel a total distance of nearly 100 kilometres. However, the astronauts never drove more than ten kilometres from the **lunar module** in case anything went wrong and they had to walk back.

Lunar drill

Left: *The Moon buggy in action. A television camera keeps an eye on the astronauts, and the aerial shaped like an inside-out umbrella transmits its picture back to Earth.*

Above each wheel was what looked like a mudguard. There is no mud on the Moon—because there is no water there—and the wheel covers were to stop Moon dust being sprayed by the wheels onto the astronauts and their **equipment**.

The astronauts had no steering wheel but a set of levers that controlled the speed of each wheel. They could not get lost, no matter where they went. Before them was a **display panel** that always told them where the lunar module was and how far from it the astronauts were. Also, the buggy was always in contact with Earth. At the back there was an aerial which looked like an umbrella turned inside out to send radio and television **signals** back to Earth.

By guiding the colour television camera on the buggy, **mission control** on Earth could watch the astronauts.

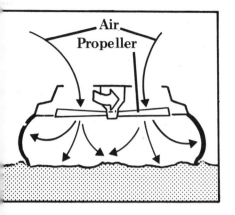

Air Propeller

Above: *Air is forced under the hull, filling out the 'skirt' and lifting the craft.* **Below:** *A sea-going hovercraft moving off the slipway onto the sea.*

Travelling on Air

To many people who are used to flying by aircraft to distant places, going by boat can seem to take for ever. The boat lumbers through the waves, unable to go much faster than about 50 kilometres an hour. The power of the engine is taken up in pushing the water aside, and the only way to move faster is to raise the **hull** above the water. The fastest passenger-carrying watercraft—the hovercraft and hydrofoil—both work in this way, cutting travelling time by half.

The hovercraft raises itself above the water by forcing air beneath its hull to make a cushion of air between the hull and the water. A **flexible** 'skirt' surrounds the hull to stop the air immediately escaping. The hovercraft rests on the air cushion, raised a few centimetres above the surface of the water. It pushes itself over the waves either with airscrews like the **propellers** on aircraft, or by means of a long propeller

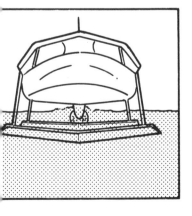

that dips beneath the hull into the water. One advantage of having airscrews to move the hovercraft is that the machine can travel up a ramp out of the water or it can land on a beach. It can also travel easily over swamps and marshes. **Expeditions** have used the hovercraft to explore remote parts of the world by travelling up rivers and over lakes and swamps.

A hydrofoil raises its hull out of the water by having a wing-shaped blade fixed beneath it. As it begins to move through the water, the blade rises and pushes the hull out of the water.

Riding in both a hovercraft and a hydrofoil is more like a trip in an aircraft than a boat. The cabin is completely enclosed, for you cannot go outside, and you look out of the windows through a cloud of spray as you speed over the waves.

145

Giants of the Sea

The world's greatest ships used to be the glamorous ocean liners. They sailed the world's oceans like huge floating hotels, providing their passengers with everything they could want—restaurants, bars, swimming pools, shops, a theatre, a library, even a hospital in case of emergencies. But air travel has brought about the end of most ocean travel, and the few liners that are left look small beside today's huge supertankers. The largest of the supertankers is more than five times as large as the greatest ocean liner and even bigger supertankers are being built.

Supertankers usually carry oil, though some may carry other kinds of **cargo**. Some years ago, shipbuilders realized that the larger a ship is, the more cheaply it can carry cargo. Just about every country in the world needs oil, so the demand for it is very great. A new source of oil is the recently developed oil deposits beneath the world's oceans. This new resource has resulted in the development of the giant oil platform and the undersea pipeline.

At the time of writing, the world's largest tanker is the *Globtik London,* which sails between the Persian Gulf and Japan carrying a cargo of about 580 million litres of oil on each voyage. When it is unloaded, it weighs 483,939 tonnes and is 379 metres long. Its deck is so vast that it could hold 79 tennis courts side by side. But a **crew** of only 38 people is needed to sail this giant across the sea, for the ship has automatic **navigation** aids that do most of the work.

However, by the time you read this, the record for the largest ship will probably have passed to even greater supertankers of more than 500,000 tonnes.

Left: *The 379-metre-long tanker is only a few metres shorter than the tallest building in the world—the Sears Roebuck building in Chicago, U.S.A. (see pages 122 and 123).*

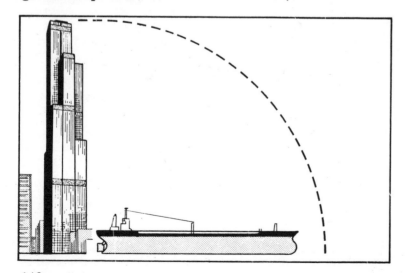

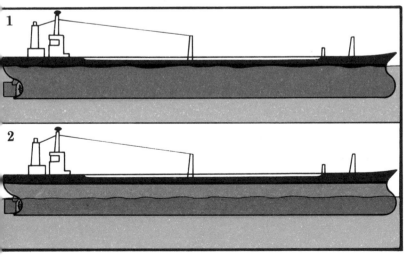

Above: *The supertanker* Globtik London, *the largest ship in the world at the moment.* **Left:** *When fully loaded, most of the hull of a supertanker lies beneath the waterline (1). Unloaded, it floats half out of the water (2).*

Fastest Thing on Wheels

In his attempts to find faster means of transport, man has always raced. First animals and then machines have been used to find the fastest way of travelling. **Ice yachts** beat horses, and then the speed record went to railway engines, followed by aircraft and now spacecraft —although a downhill skier did become the world's fastest man from 1873 to 1890. At no time has the record been held by anyone driving a car or a boat. However, the spacecraft speed record of nearly 40,000 kilometres an hour is now unlikely to become any faster until a different kind of spacecraft is invented. The excitement remains on land and water, mainly because such record attempts are highly dangerous.

    Piston engines and **propellers** are no longer able to drive cars and boats to the highest speeds. Instead, jet

Below: *The Blue Flame, the world's fastest car. Powered by a liquid gas rocket engine, the car has exceeded 1000 kilometres an hour, and could possibly go even faster. The record run took place in 1970 on the Bonneville Salt Flats, Utah, U.S.A.*

engines have been used. A jet-powered boat reached a speed of more than 500 kilometres an hour on Lake Coniston in 1967. But suddenly the boat rose in the air and smashed into the lake, killing its driver, Donald Campbell—this is an unofficial record.

Speeding on wheels is somewhat safer. When the jet-powered car *Spirit of America* went out of control at Bonneville Salt Flats in the United States in 1964, it left skid marks nearly ten kilometres long. However, the driver, Craig Breedlove, was not killed, and a year later he set up a record of nearly 1,000 kilometres an hour. This was beaten in 1970 by Gary Gabelich in his rocket-powered car *The Blue Flame*, which reached 1,016 kilometres an hour. In fact, the car is powerful enough to go even faster, but it might then break the sound barrier and no one knows exactly what would happen. However, someone is going to find out before very long!

Travelling in a Tube

If everyone who had to enter a city—either to work, shop or look at its sights—travelled by road, then traffic jams would block every main street and the city would come to a standstill. With an underground railway, great numbers of people can travel to any part of the city quickly; in fact you could travel from one side of the city to the other and never need to come to the surface, though it might not be as comfortable as a car.

In New York, for example 2,000 million journeys are made on the underground railway every year. If everyone makes one return journey a day, this means that an average of three million people travel on the subway every day.

Automatic machinery helps to make travelling on an underground railway fast and safe. Ticket machines in the entrance hall of the station give a ticket on putting in a coin—often giving change if it is needed. The ticket may have a **magnetic** coating which has an identification pattern. The passenger goes to an automatic gate and puts his ticket into a slot. The gate 'reads' the ticket and opens for the passenger as it returns the ticket. The passenger than takes an escalator or lift—again driven automatically—to the platform.

The train itself may be guided electronically. Although there is a driver sitting in front, on some trains he merely presses a button to start the train when everyone is aboard. The train then travels automatically to the next station as quickly as possible. No driver could safely guide a train through the dark tunnels of an underground **system**, and so all the signals are automatic. The track is divided into sections that may be occupied by only one train at a time. If another train approaches an occupied section, its brakes are automatically switched on and it cannot enter until the train in front has gone. This is why an underground train sometimes stops in the tunnel before reaching a station.

Several new developments have been made on underground systems to improve travel. Some trains have air conditioning and rubber wheels to make the journey comfortable and quiet. Loudspeakers in the coaches mean that the driver can make announcements.

Right: *A honeycomb of tunnels lies beneath a busy London street. At this station there are two different lines, one underneath the other. Escalators take passengers from one platform to another and on up to the surface.*

Opposite page: *An experimental design for a small hover-train. The train runs on a raised track and if it comes into service could carry passengers at high speed from one city to another.*
Below: *The French Aérotrain, a fast, experimental hover-train.*

Half Train, Half Plane

There was a time when travelling on the railway was much faster than going by car. But the building of motorways (you can read about motorways on pages 52 and 53) and the use of faster aircraft mean going by train is not always the quickest way to travel. With new high-speed trains, it could be just as quick to take a train from one city centre to another as to fly. Trains can only be made faster by taking away their wheels, because **friction** with the track limits speeds. By hovering above the track instead of touching it, a train could reach a speed of 500 kilometres an hour!

This can be done in two ways. The train could produce its own cushion of air as a hovercraft does, driven along by **propellers** or a jet engine (you can read about hovercraft on pages 144 and 145). Alternatively, the train could be suspended just above the track by a **magnetic field** and moved by a **linear induction motor.** The motor pushes the train magnetically along the track, it is completely silent and the most likely to be used. In both cases the train does not touch the ground. It moves through the air, just as an aircraft does. With air travel, more time is often spent travelling from the city centre to the airport than in the air. The high-speed train would go directly from one city centre to the other, saving much time and trouble.

WONDERFUL
MATERIALS

Prehistoric man could make things only from the materials he found around him. Wood, stone, clay, plant fibres, skins, fur and bone had to serve his every need. Then a great advance was made—metals were discovered. About a hundred years ago, through an understanding of chemistry, ways to make new materials completely unlike those found in nature were discovered. These wonderful new materials, which include synthetic fibres like the woven polypropylene shown below, have improved our lives in many ways.

Getting it Together

Mending a broken chair, pasting up wallpaper, licking an envelope to stick it down, binding a parcel with adhesive tape, placing a plaster over a cut—each of these everyday actions needs a particular kind of adhesive or glue. Some adhesives have to be strong—the mended chair should not fall apart nor the envelope come open in the post. But other adhesives must be quite weak—wallpaper will eventually have to be replaced and the sticky plaster must come away from the skin without damage to the wound.

The very strongest adhesives are called epoxy resins and they form bonds that are even stronger than the materials they join. This means that any **structure**

Opposite page: *The goal-keeper has been stuck to the crossbar with epoxy resin adhesive on the soles of his boots.*
Right: *Because epoxy resin adhesives work by a chemical reaction and do not need air to harden, they will even work under water.*

joined by the adhesive is not weak at the joints and will not break there. Epoxy resins are used to glue concrete beams and panels together in buildings—the concrete shells of the Sydney Opera House are made of segments joined by epoxy adhesives (you can read about the Sydney Opera House on pages 130 and 131). Epoxies are also very useful in building because they set firm in damp conditions. By mixing the adhesive with sand or powdered stone, it can be used to repair holes in concrete and stone structures.

Adhesives are not only used to join things together. Many materials are made by sticking pieces together. The papyrus on which **scribes** wrote in ancient times was made by binding reed **fibres** with flour paste. Plywood is made of layers of wood glued together, and many kinds of artificial wood are made by binding wood chips with adhesive. Artificial stone blocks that are easy to fit together in building are made by mixing adhesives with powdered stone and forming them into stone-like blocks that can be used instead of bricks.

Materials in Space

The giant step out into the Universe that man took in 1969, when the Apollo astronauts landed on the Moon, was a dangerous venture into the unknown. Many new materials had to be developed to get the astronauts to the Moon—and bring them back safely.

The Apollo spacecraft was constructed of aluminium honeycomb, a material that is light to save fuel, yet strong enough to resist the stresses of lift-off and re-entry and the intense cold of space. Special **semiconductors** had to be developed so that the spacecraft's computers could be made small yet still able to handle the complex calculations required to **navigate** through

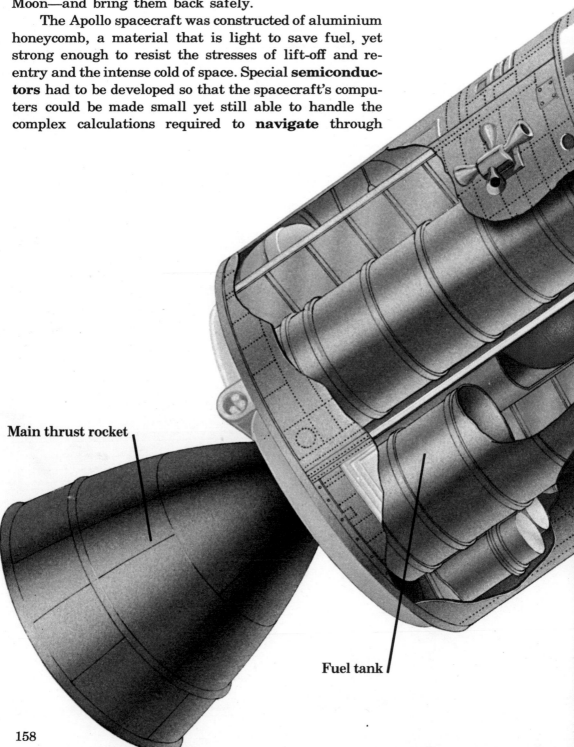

Main thrust rocket

Fuel tank

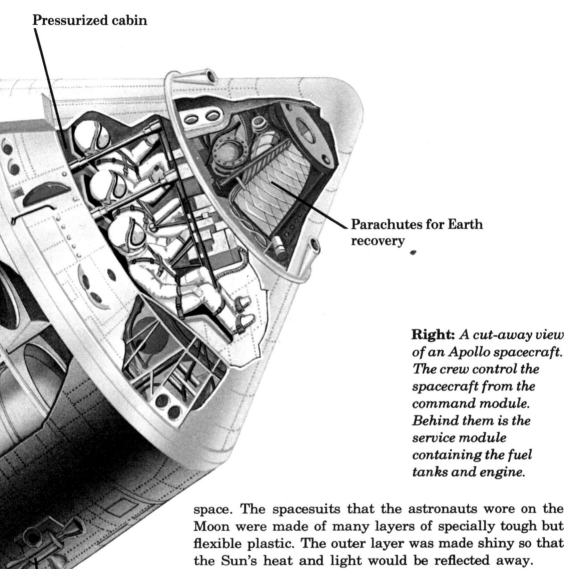

Pressurized cabin

Parachutes for Earth recovery

Small rockets for manoeuvring in space

Right: A cut-away view of an Apollo spacecraft. The crew control the spacecraft from the command module. Behind them is the service module containing the fuel tanks and engine.

space. The spacesuits that the astronauts wore on the Moon were made of many layers of specially tough but flexible plastic. The outer layer was made shiny so that the Sun's heat and light would be reflected away.

Inside the spacecraft, special food was needed to make eating easy in the weightless conditions. Some of the food was specially dried and placed in plastic bags. When he came to eat, the astronaut squirted some hot or cold water into the bag, squeezed the bag to mix the food and water together, and then sucked it into his mouth.

Getting astronauts safely back to Earth presents a big problem. The spacecraft, on re-entering the Earth's atmosphere, is subjected to fantastic heat. But the base of the spacecraft has a heat shield made of steel honeycomb and hard epoxy resin (you can read about epoxy resin on pages 156 and 157). As the spacecraft enters the atmosphere on its return from space, the resin heats up and flakes away, leaving the main structure of the spacecraft unharmed.

Strength with Lightness

Many materials are strong and many are light, but few are both. It is these kinds of materials that makers of sailing boats and racing cars look for. A light vehicle needs less power to move. One of the best materials to use is one that is the most unexpected—glass. Not as panes of glass, which break too easily, but as **fibres.**

Glass fibre is a strong fibre. To make racing cars and sailing boats, plastics (you can read about plastics on pages 166 and 167) are reinforced with glass fibres to make a light but very strong material that is easily shaped into a car body or a boat hull. This is done by putting a layer of glass fibre on top of a layer of liquid plastic; then another layer of glass fibre is applied, and so on, until the required thickness has been built up. Lightness is very important in racing cars and sailing boats and these are generally made of fibre-glass reinforced plastics.

Above: *A racing car with a body made of fibre-glass.*

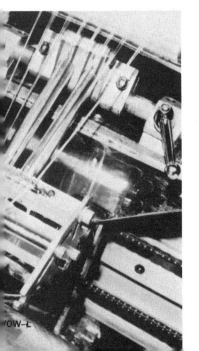

Below: *Glass fibres being spun from strands of molten glass.*

There are other good reasons for using fibre-glass reinforced plastics. The material does not rust and needs little looking after. If the car body or boat hull should be dented or holed, the damage is quickly repaired by filling in with more fibre-glass reinforced plastic. Other uses for this material include tools and aircraft parts. Some **sculptors** work in fibre-glass reinforced plastics. It is easy to colour the material by adding the colour to the plastic when it sets into shape.

Another important use for glass fibres is to make glass wool or **yarn.** Glass wool is good for retaining heat because it contains trapped pockets of air. The roofs of modern houses are lined with glass wool to stop heat escaping and so the cost of heating is less. Glass **fabrics** can be made by weaving glass-fibre yarn. These fabrics are strong and will not burn. They are used to make fireproof curtains and bullet-proof jackets.

Glass fibres are made by heating glass rods and pulling them out into threads, or by forcing melted glass through small holes to produce fibres of glass.

161

Knitted Steaks

Many of the world's people spend their lives in hunger and suffering with illness caused by shortage of food. This problem is likely to get worse rather than better as the number of people in the world gets larger all the time. The reason is that keeping animals for meat uses up a lot of land that could be used to grow **crops.** A field of spinach, for example, can feed over 20 times more people than the same field used to keep animals for meat.

Meat is good for us because it contains **protein,** which we need to keep healthy. However, plants also contain protein, and one plant, the soya bean, contains more protein than meat does. Ways have been found of making artificial meat from the protein in the soya bean. If people will eat the artificial meat, then the land can be used to feed far more people.

One problem is that soya protein does not taste or look like meat. The protein has therefore to be made to look like meat and flavoured to taste like meat. This is

Right: *These chunks of 'meat' are made entirely of artificial protein called 'Kesp'.*
Opposite page: *The hamburger, the filling in the pie, the sausages and the stuffing in the tomatoes are all made from soya bean protein.*

done in much the same way that artificial fibres are made and turned into cloth (you can read about artificial fibres on pages 164 and 165). Artificial meat is therefore often known as 'knitted steaks'.

The soya protein is dissolved in an **alkali** and then made into fibres by forcing this protein mixture into a bath of acid and salt, where it sets into threads. The threads are wound onto reels and washed. Then they are mixed with fats, flavours, colouring and **nutrients** and bound together with a protein binder (usually white of egg). The blended fibres can then be shaped not only into steaks but into granules, cubes and slices. These can be used to make stews, casseroles, curries and meat sauces. The food is just as good for you as real meat dishes and tastes the same.

New Clothes for Old

Until fairly recently many people had to live their lives serving others. Poor servants had to clean, cook and wash clothes for their rich masters. If they could be brought from the past to our time, they would be amazed by all the changes.

The most obvious changes would be the use of machines to do work and the improved health of people. Our time travellers would probably also gasp at the new styles of clothes, but they would not remark upon the materials being worn. To them it would look as if everyone was still wearing clothes made from natural wool and cotton. But here, too, our visitors would find that life had become easier, for, however natural most of

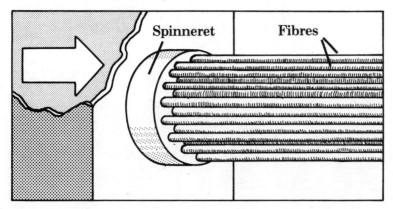

Spinneret   Fibres

Left: *Most artificial fibres are made by forcing a plastic in liquid form (such as nylon) through tiny holes. The fibres harden and are then wound on to reels.*

our materials look, many of them are quite different when it comes to washing and wearing them. Most do not need ironing after washing; some can stretch without becoming baggy; others are hard-wearing yet soft; many are light yet warm; and most cost less than natural materials.

These modern fabrics differ from those of yesteryear because they are woven from artificial fibres—fibres made entirely by man rather than the traditional fibres gathered from plants and animal fur. Many clothes are made of mixtures of both natural and artificial fibres. Most man-made fibres are made of thin threads of plastic such as nylon, but others, such as rayon, are made from natural substances and changed by man by adding certain chemicals. Clothes are not the only way we can use these man-made fibres. Hard-wearing carpets, strong ropes and safety belts, and tough strings for musical instruments are other examples. Glass fibres are used in plastics to add strength, and they are also woven into insulating materials.

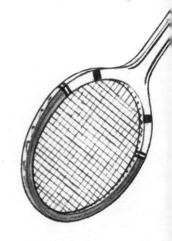

164

Jumper: *Wool and nylon mixture.*
T. Shirt: *Polyester and cotton mixture.*
Jacket: *Fun fur, made of acrylic fibre.*
Shorts and Trousers: *Polyester fibre.*
Socks: *Nylon.*

All the clothes that the two children are wearing are either made completely from artificial fibre, or are a mixture of natural and artificial fibres. A man-made fibre is also used to manufacture the strings on the tennis racket.

165

Plastic—The All-Purpose Material

Until recently a bucket could only be made of metal or possibly leather, a cup of **ceramic**, a chair of wood. Now chemists have developed ways of making new materials totally unlike those we get from nature. Artificial dyes give us colours that do not fade. New drugs have completely changed medicine.

In 1909 a Belgian chemist called Dr. Leo Baekland combined two cheap chemicals together and formed a completely new substance. It was called Bakelite, after its inventor, and was the world's first plastic. Unlike today's brightly coloured plastics, Bakelite was naturally very dark in colour. It was widely used for such things as door handles, radio cabinets and ash trays, but today it is hardly used at all.

The modern plastics are very useful, because they are so easy to shape into new objects. A bucket, cup and even a chair can be made in a second, simply by stamping them out of a piece of plastic in a moulding machine.

Polyvinyl chloride (PVC) is a rubbery plastic used to make gramophone records, boots and dolls.

Polyethylene is either flexible or rigid and used to make plastic film and bottles.

Cellulose acetate is used in making photographic film as well as toothbrushes.

166

Plastics can be as hard and tough as metal and wood, as transparent as glass, as light and soft as the finest cloth, as flexible as rubber or sponge. And unlike natural materials, they cannot rot, rust or tarnish and can be made unbreakable. Plastics have therefore come to be used for all kinds of everyday objects and, being so much cheaper and easier to use than natural materials, have made life much more comfortable.

Plastics are made by substances produced from oil and coal. They are not only replacements for natural materials, for many modern developments would have been impossible without plastics. The recording and cinema industries could not have developed without plastics to make records, tapes and films. Modern non-drip and quick-drying paints are produced from liquid plastics, and crease-resistant and non-iron fabrics are woven from plastic fibres.

Early plastics were virtually indestructible; that means that we could never completely destroy a plastic object, there would always be something left. Recently plastic has been made so that it is reduced to dust when it is subjected to a very strong light.

Polypropylene is a very strong plastic and used to make modern furniture, toys and many kinds of kitchen containers.

Polyurethane is contained in tough high-gloss paints and varnishes.

Polystyrene plastics are heat resistant and used in the manufacture of containers of many kinds, as well as tiles.

THE WONDERFUL ART OF HEALING

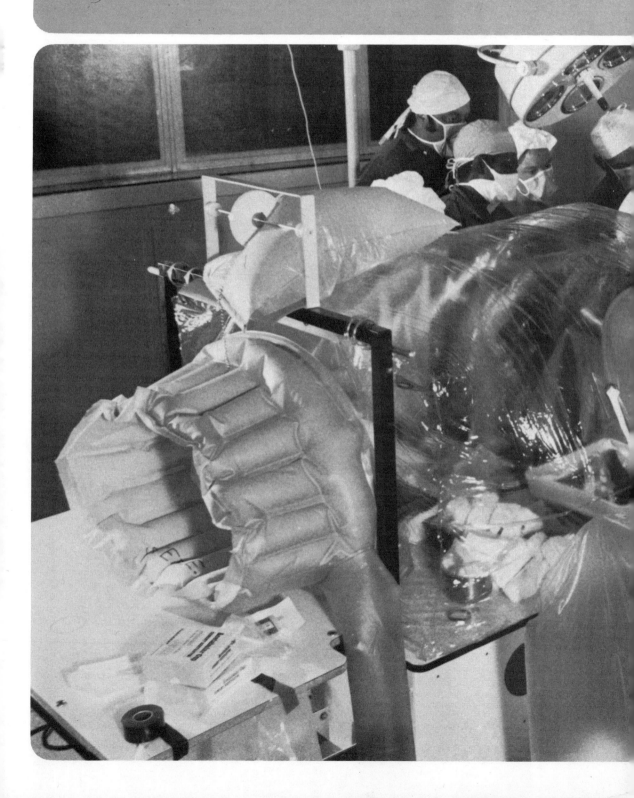

Modern medicine is perhaps the greatest gift that science has given us. No longer need we fear pain, disease or disability. Many of us will live a full and long life. Cleanliness is the key to good health. The operating theatre of a hospital has to be kept as clean as possible to stop germs causing infection. Below: A patient lies under an inflated plastic bag that is completely free of germs. To perform the operation, the surgeon reaches into glove-shaped armholes in the envelope, so that his fingers are sealed in a thin covering of germ-free plastic.

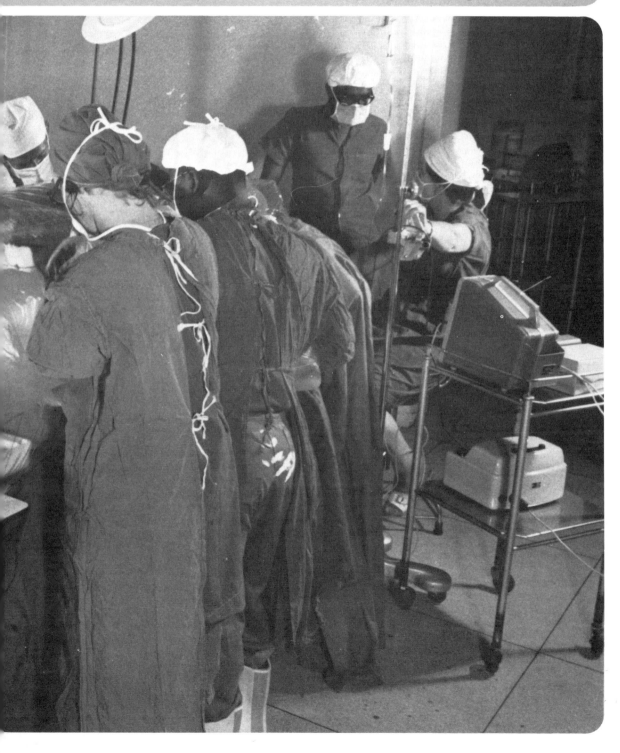

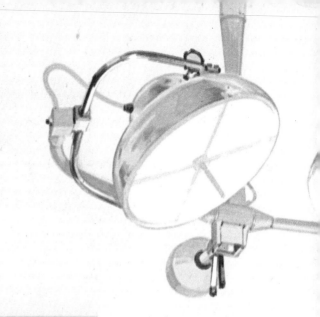

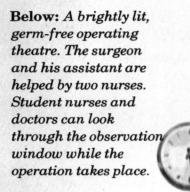

Below: *A brightly lit, germ-free operating theatre. The surgeon and his assistant are helped by two nurses. Student nurses and doctors can look through the observation window while the operation takes place.*

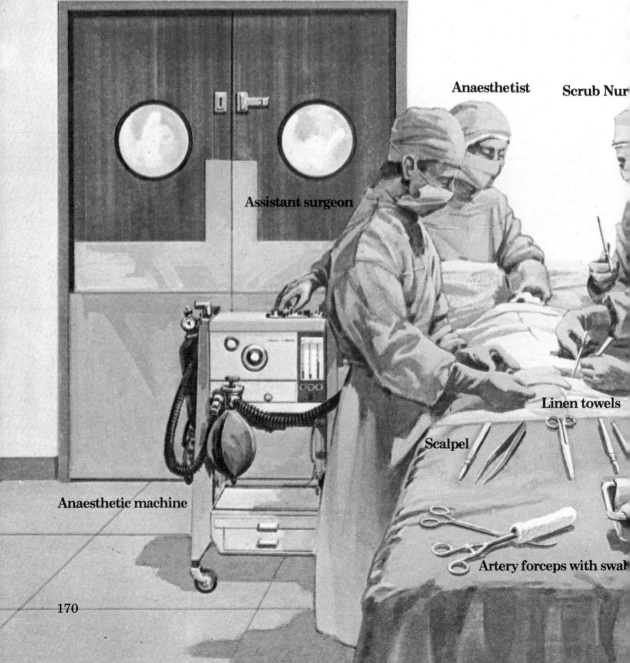

Anaesthetist

Scrub Nur

Assistant surgeon

Linen towels

Scalpel

Anaesthetic machine

Artery forceps with swa

The Operating Theatre

Some of us will have to have an operation at some time in our lives. Damage to the body has to be repaired, often to save life. During an operation you will be under great care. However, you will not know anything about it. **Anaesthetics** keep you asleep so that you feel no pain. The anaesthetist makes sure that you stay asleep and keep breathing properly the whole time.

The surgeons carry out the operation, helped by nurses who prepare and hand them the instruments they need. Everyone wears special masks and gowns and the whole theatre and its air are kept free of germs to stop infection entering your body. You lie on an operating table beneath bright lights and surrounded by machines. In very bad illnesses a machine can take over from the heart and the lungs while the operation is carried out.

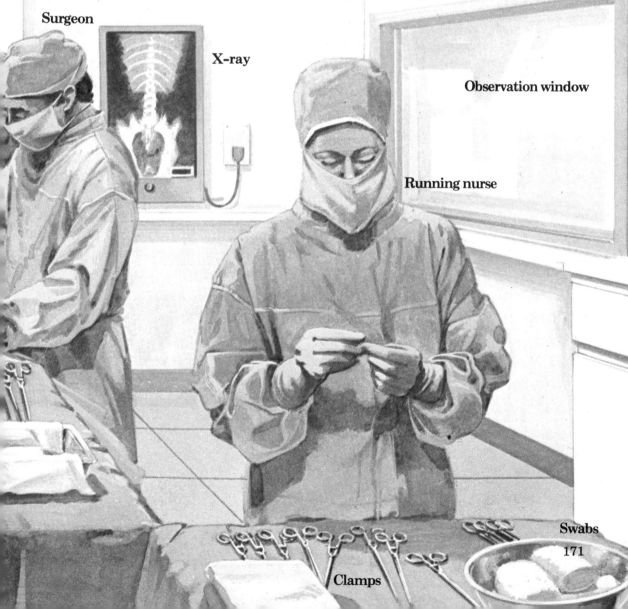

Surgeon

X-ray

Observation window

Running nurse

Swabs

Clamps

Getting the Needle

One of the strangest, yet best ways of stopping pain was invented in China thousands of years ago. But it is hardly used in the western part of the world. This is acupuncture. In China, if anyone is suffering from pain for any reason, he or she can go to an acupuncturist. The acupuncturist will examine the patient and place needles into the skin in certain parts of the body. The pain then disappears. Even the most unbearable pain can disappear with acupuncture. In China, people having operations (you can read about the operating theatre on pages 170 and 171) in which the body is cut open may have acupuncture instead of an **anaesthetic**. They remain awake during the operation and feel no pain.

It might seem that the needles going into the skin hurt so much that the patient cannot feel anything else,

Opposite page: *The acupuncture points on the hands. There are many more points all over the body.*
Below: *A patient who suffers from hay-fever undergoes treatment by acupuncture. Each session takes half-an-hour and prevents hay-fever from recurring later.*

but this is not true, the needles are short and go in just below the surface. The patient feels a slight prick as they go in, and then is perfectly comfortable. The needles are not put in at the actual point of pain. Instead they are inserted in special parts of the body depending on the kind of illness the patient has. It is possible that acupuncture kills pain by interfering with the nerves and preventing them from carrying pain signals from an injury or painful part of the body to the brain. Even though we do feel pain in different parts of the body, it is in fact our brain that makes us feel the pain.

Acupuncture is not a cure for the illness itself or whatever it is that is causing pain. Instead, acupuncture may take away the symptoms. Symptoms are the pain and distress that illnesses make you feel. Unfortunately, no one can be absolutely sure that acupuncture will always work.

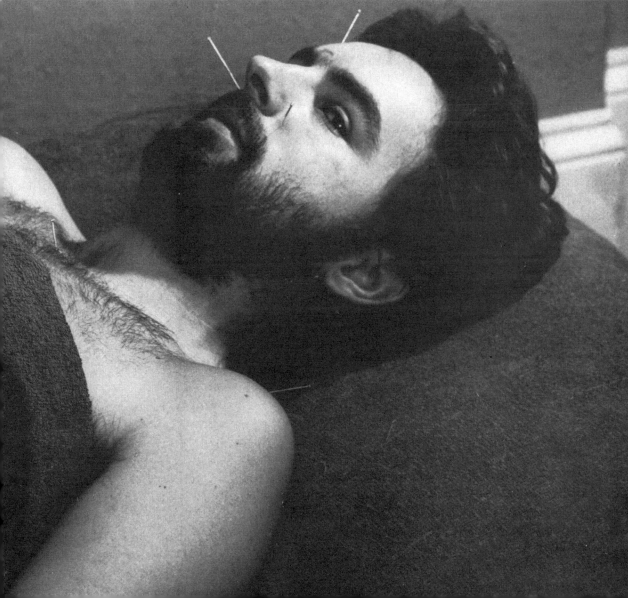

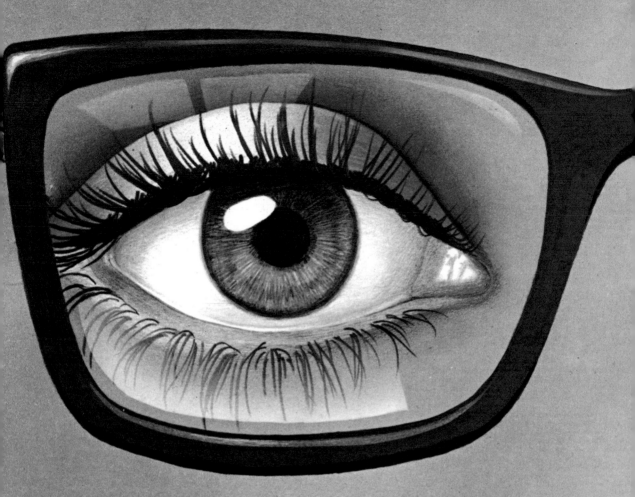

Invisible Glasses

'Nobody's perfect' is a saying we often use. No one person has sharp vision, acute hearing, sensitive touch, and delicate senses of smell and taste. At least one of these senses is usually less than perfect. But the most obviously affected are those people with poor vision who have to wear spectacles.

Wearing a pair of glasses can look very fashionable, but many people prefer to squint and stare in a vain effort to overcome their blurred vision rather than get spectacles. They may not realize that many of the people they talk to also have poor vision but can see perfectly well without glasses.

Instead, these people are wearing contact lenses—tiny plastic lenses that fit invisibly and painlessly on the eyeball. Contact lenses do not mist over in moist air as spectacles can do. Contact lenses will correct certain

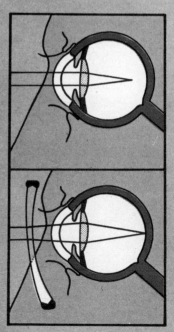

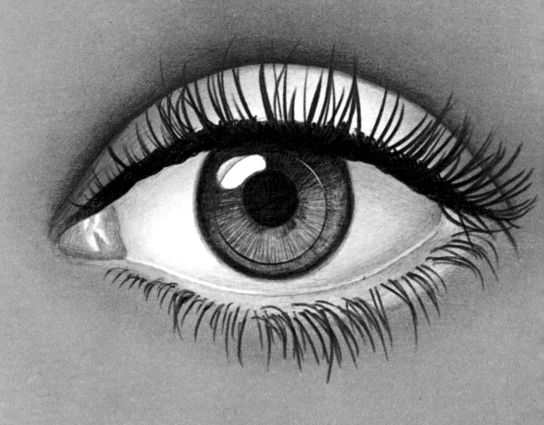

Above: *A contact lens (right) can correct sight just as well as a spectacle lens (left), but is invisible in use.*
Left, top: *Bad sight occurs when the lens in the eye wrongly focuses light rays that have come from an object.*
Left, below: *To correct this, another lens is needed. This extra lens focuses the light rays correctly on the retina at the back of the eye.*

kinds of poor vision that spectacles cannot improve. And if you want to change the colour of your eyes—as actors may do—then all you have to do is wear coloured contact lenses. However, not all defects of vision can be corrected by contact lenses and some people find them uncomfortable to wear as they irritate their eyes and make it even more difficult to see.

Even a person with good eyesight may have to put on glasses when the sun is shining brightly—in this case, sunglasses. These are usually made of ordinary glass that has been coloured, but many people who normally wear glasses have a second pair with dark lenses for bright sunlight. Now the inconvenience of carrying two pairs of spectacles can be overcome by having one pair made of photochromatic glass instead. This glass darkens when the Sun shines and clears when the light becomes dim, letting the right amount of light through all the time, so that the eyes never strain.

Seeing Through People

Doctors in the past must have longed for a machine that would let them see inside people. Only then could they be sure of finding out what was wrong with many of their **patients.** In this century, we have discovered several ways of seeing into people. The first and most important way is to use X-rays. These rays go through flesh in exactly the same way as light goes through glass. But they do not go easily through bone. If a photograph is taken of part of the body with X-rays, then the flesh hardly shows at all, but the bones stand out. The parts inside the body show up, and doctors can see what is

Opposite page: *This enlargement of an X-ray photograph of a hand shows clearly the various bones in the hand. On one finger, the metal band of a ring stands out sharply.*
Right: *An X-ray photograph is made of a patient's hip. Every hospital has an X-ray department to help the doctors find out what is wrong.*

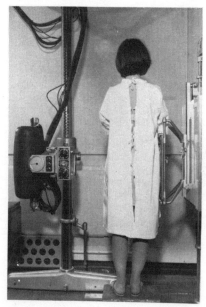

wrong and know exactly what to do to help a patient. Dentists use X-rays too. X-ray pictures of the teeth show up any decay that needs to be treated before the teeth get so bad that they begin to hurt.

However, X-rays begin to harm the body if they are given too often. Doctors therefore have other ways of seeing into the body. One way is to use tiny cameras fixed onto long **flexible** rods that can actually go into the body to take a look around (you can read about these rods on pages 202 and 203). Another way is to use ultrasonic sound instead of X-rays. This kind of sound is far too high for humans to hear, but it can be used to bounce off things inside the body and give a picture in much the same way as radar works (you can read about radar on pages 192 and 193). Babies are often looked at in this way before they are born!

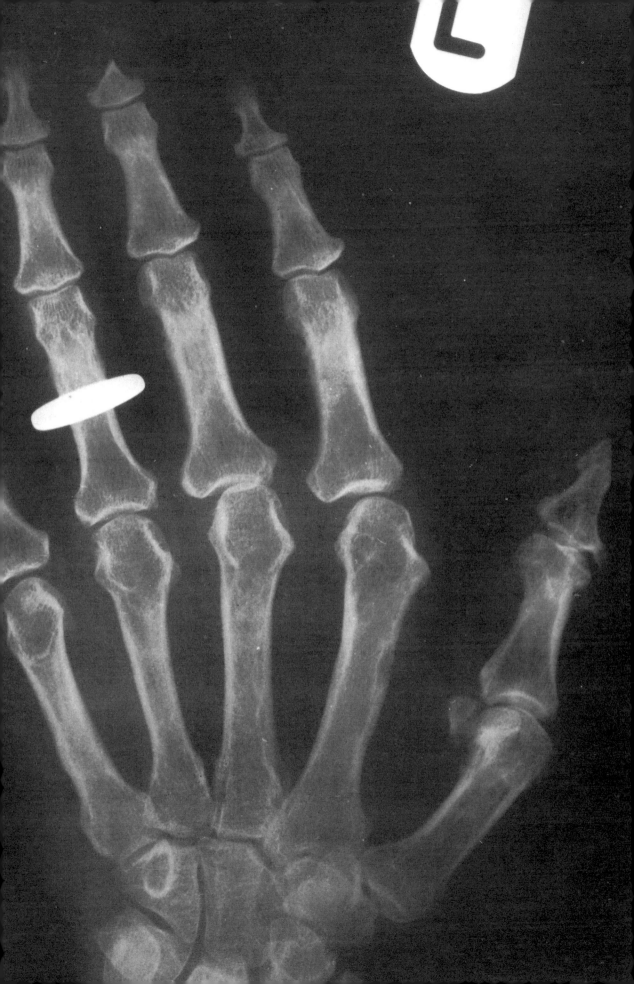

Wonderful pills

Freedom from pain is perhaps the greatest freedom that we can enjoy. **Anaesthetics** remove the pain from surgery and dentistry, and one of the first acts a doctor will do when arriving at an accident is to try to ease the pain of the victims. And we can easily treat the pain of such minor **ailments** as headache, toothache and stomach ache without even troubling the doctor. Swallowing a couple of pain-killing tablets is all we need to do to make the pain go away.

This great gift to our lives has been with us for only a century. Before then, people had to suffer very much. But they did have some **remedies**. To reduce pain and fever, Hippocrates—the ancient Greek doctor often called the father of medicine—made his patients chew willow bark. This remedy worked and continued to be used. Then about a century ago a substance called salicin was found in willow bark. This was found to take away pain, and from it a better pain killer called acetyl-salicylic acid was made and given the popular name of aspirin. It is now used throughout the world as a pain killer, and a hundred tonnes of it are manufactured every day.

Above: *Soluble aspirin tablets quickly dissolve in water.* **Right:** *When the solution is swallowed, it goes to the stomach. From there, the pain-killing ingredients enter the bloodstream and travel to the brain, where they act to stop the pain.*

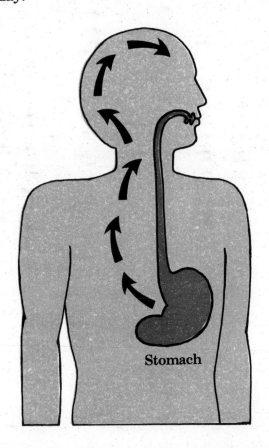

Stomach

178

Many traditional remedies actually do work for good scientific reasons. The expression 'an apple a day keeps the doctor away' is good advice to all, as fresh fruit helps to keep you healthy. In 1747, a Scottish doctor named James Lind found that a disease called scurvy, from which sailors often suffered, could be treated with fresh citrus fruits such as oranges. The sailors got scurvy because their ships carried no fruit.

The treatment worked because most fruits contain a substance known as ascorbic acid. A small amount of this substance must be present in our food, otherwise we get scurvy. Several other substances are also necessary to prevent disease, and these substances are known as vitamins. Vitamin pills contain the vitamins we need to keep healthy, and it is a good idea to take them regularly in case your diet lacks any of them. Also, ascorbic acid (vitamin C) can help to prevent colds.

Below: *This single pill contains as much vitamin C as six oranges.*

Right: *The face of a man before he undergoes a face lift by plastic surgery.*

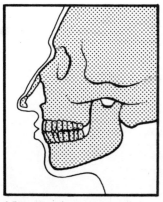

Above: *A cross section of a 'Roman' nose before the man has surgery.*

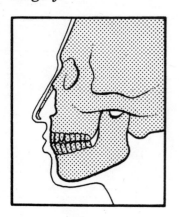

Above: *After surgery the nose has been straightened and made smaller by removing some bone and tissue.*

Putting on a New Face

Bad accidents often leave ugly scars when the wounds heal, and people are sometimes born with their faces spoilt by a harelip or cleft palate, which do not look very nice and make it difficult to speak clearly. Burns leave puckered areas of skin that their owners may often try to hide. Even people who have not suffered in these ways may consider themselves born ugly, especially if they have a birthmark, or feel that they are losing their looks as they get older.

Before the 20th century, doctors had tried to help injured people but they had little success. After World War I there were many more doctors specializing in a new type of medicine we call plastic surgery. It is called plastic surgery, not because it uses plastics, but because plastic really means shaping or moulding. A plastic

Left: *The man's face after plastic surgery. The wrinkles in the forehead and around the eyes have been removed by pulling back the skin and removing a fold. The ears, which used to stick out, have been pulled back. The nose has been straightened and made smaller. The folds of skin around the chin have been reduced.*

surgeon reshapes the body.

To remove scars or marked areas of skin the plastic surgeon may make a skin graft. This is a simple operation, in which a thin layer of skin is taken from one part of the body and sewn to the part of skin being repaired. The layer grows in place of the scarred or marked skin, and new skin grows again in the place from where the skin was taken.

Plastic surgeons can also reshape parts of the face and the rest of the body if they are damaged. Bones can be reshaped and pieces of tissue moved from one part of the body to another.

Plastic surgery can be used to make people's faces look better—changing the shape of noses or ears and removing folds of skin. This operation is often called a face-lift, or cosmetic surgery, but most plastic surgeons will only do this when really necessary.

HELPING MAN

We can live comfortable lives nowadays because there are machines that can work for us. Helped by machines, each one of us can do more work and so earn more money. Or, as with the labour-saving gadgets of a modern kitchen, shown in the picture below, we can spend less time working and have more time to ourselves and with our families. Machines may also extend our senses and our abilities—radar enables us to peer through fog and calculators help us to do very complicated arithmetic quickly.

Mechanical Muscles

Man could not have made the tremendous technological advances he has made if he had not long ago invented machines that would lift and carry things for him. The Ancient Greek scientist Archimedes, who lived about 200 B.C., first worked out that levers and **pulleys** could magnify man's muscle power. He is supposed to have built a pulley system with which a man could haul a ship onto the shore single-handed!

But such efforts would have appeared small beside the strength of today's giant mechanical slaves. The most powerful crane in the world can lift a weight of nearly 2,000 tonnes. Strangely enough, this is not a huge crane that towers over the ground, but is mounted on a ship and helps with the building of oil rigs at sea. The tallest land-based crane is a mobile one, 202 metres high, but for all its height it can only lift 1000 tonnes, only half that of the ship-mounted crane.

Helicopters can lift up to 40 tonnes and are often used instead of cranes. Church steeples can be easily lifted into position by a helicopter. The most unusual carrying vehicle is the huge crawler that transported *Saturn V* Moon rockets from the assembly building to the launching pad at the Kennedy Space Center in Florida. The world's most massive vehicle, the Saturn rocket crawler is 40 metres long.

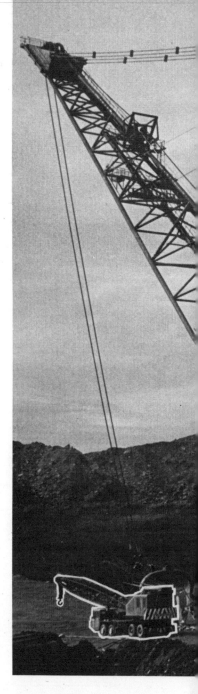

Left: *The crawler that carried the* Saturn V *Moon rocket to its launching pad is the most massive vehicle that has ever been built. It weighs more than 8,000 tonnes when loaded, and it has the largest windscreen wipers in the world—more than a metre long.*

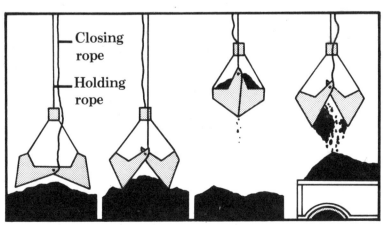

Closing
rope

Holding
rope

Above: *'Big Geordie',
the biggest crane in
Europe, compared with
a normal sized crane.
This giant crane is used
in the British coal
industry.*
Left: *Two ropes support
the grab of a crane, one
to lift and one to close it.*

The Combine Harvester

Harvesting was once a back-breaking job, as farmers had to work with a **scythe** or a **sickle** to cut the golden wheat, then separate the grain from the heads of the wheat by hand. A large group of people would work their way through the fields, cutting the wheat during all the hours of the long summer days to get the **harvest** in before the weather changed.

Nowadays, one man can gather as much wheat as the eye can see with the help of the combine harvester. This machine moves through a field of wheat, picking up the crop as it goes. Inside, the threshing parts of the machine rub and comb the heads of wheat to separate the grain from the straw. Then the mixture of grain and straw passes over shaking screens, and because the grain is small it falls through, while the straw stays on top of the screen. A blast of air blows away chaff (small pieces of straw) from the grain, and the clean grain is then

Engine

Comb and feed screw

Rotating feed

Cutters

Guides

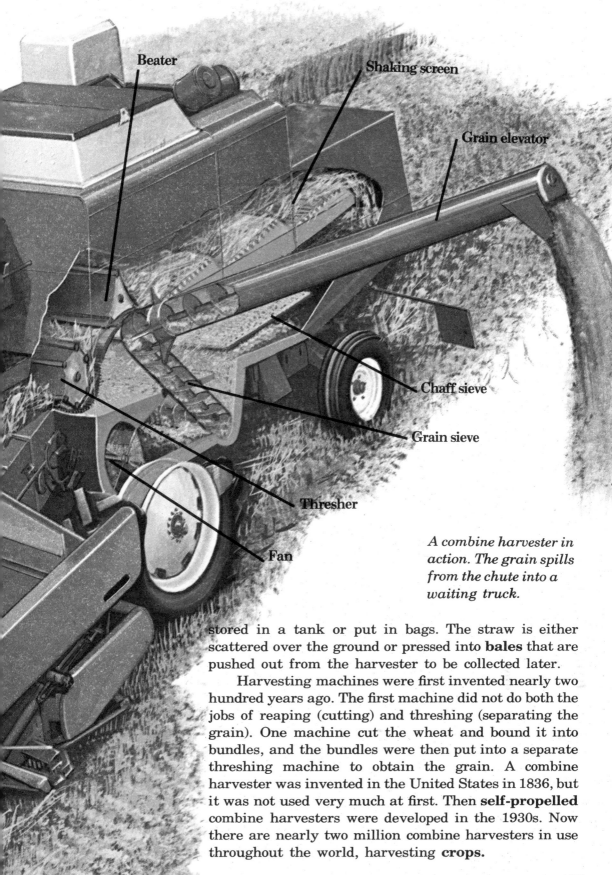

Beater

Shaking screen

Grain elevator

Chaff sieve

Grain sieve

Thresher

Fan

A combine harvester in action. The grain spills from the chute into a waiting truck.

stored in a tank or put in bags. The straw is either scattered over the ground or pressed into **bales** that are pushed out from the harvester to be collected later.

Harvesting machines were first invented nearly two hundred years ago. The first machine did not do both the jobs of reaping (cutting) and threshing (separating the grain). One machine cut the wheat and bound it into bundles, and the bundles were then put into a separate threshing machine to obtain the grain. A combine harvester was invented in the United States in 1836, but it was not used very much at first. Then **self-propelled** combine harvesters were developed in the 1930s. Now there are nearly two million combine harvesters in use throughout the world, harvesting **crops.**

As Free as a Fish

Many people have dreamed of being as free as a bird, and some have even tried strapping wings to their arms and launching themselves into the air—only to crash. However, there is one way in which almost everyone can get the feeling of flying, and that is in the sea.

Using an aqualung to breathe under water and flippers to swim powerfully, you can travel in any direction. The deepest you can go with an aqualung is about 100 metres. If you go this deep you have to surface very slowly otherwise you can be killed by the 'bends'. This is caused by gasses in the blood-stream bubbling as the diver comes up.

Diving with an aqualung is safe, as long as you learn how to use the equipment at a diving club. The aqualung is a bottle of compressed air and a **device** that makes

Below: *A man swims through the sea with an aqualung, producing a huge cloud of bubbles every time he breathes out. He is wearing weights around his waist to help him stay down. A knife is strapped to his leg in case of emergencies.*

sure air comes through the mouthpiece whenever you breathe in. The aqualung was invented by the famous French underwater explorer Jacques Cousteau. Using aqualungs, many people have discovered the secrets of the sea, and studied and photographed the strange creatures and plants to be found there, as well as exploring ancient wrecks and recovering their treasures.

Divers using the aqualung cannot go very deep. A special underwater vessel known as a bathyscaphe is needed to go deep into the darkness of the sea bottom. The bathyscaphe has a small cabin fixed beneath a large float. Air is released from tanks to reduce **buoyancy** and allows the bathyscaphe to sink. Weights are released to stop the bathyscaphe going deeper or to allow the bathyscaphe to rise to the surface. In 1960 a bathyscaphe descended eleven kilometres to the very deepest part of the ocean.

Below: *A diving bell being lowered into the sea to be used by divers. The diving bell was invented in 1599. A further development of the diving bell was the observation chamber. Italian divers used observation chambers 121 metres under the sea when they recovered a million pounds of treasure from a wreck.*

Jumping for It

Before jet aircraft were invented, a fighter pilot would have to jump out if he got into trouble and had to abandon his plane. As his aircraft crashed to the ground, he floated down with his parachute and landed safely.

However, the high speeds of jet aircraft made jumping out impossible. The rush of the air made it hard to get out of the **cockpit,** and even if he succeeded, the pilot was likely to be blown against the tail of the plane. A new way of escape had to be found, and the ejection seat was invented at the end of World War II.

Many pilots' lives have been saved by the ejection seat. Instead of jumping out in an **emergency,** the pilot pulls a cover over his face. By doing this he sets off an explosive charge under his seat and blows away the covering of the cockpit. The whole seat, with the pilot still sitting in it, is fired up into the air well above the tail of the plane. The pilot's parachute opens above the seat, the seat falls away and the parachute lowers the pilot to the ground.

The ejection seat will not only get the pilot out of an emergency high in the air. If anything should go wrong during take-off or landing, the seat will fire him high enough to come down safely with his parachute.

The jet fighter (left) has developed engine trouble and is likely to crash, so the pilot has to get out.

The small 'drogue' parachutes open above the pilot in his seat.

After the pilot has pulled his face cover, the canopy flies off the cockpit.

The seat begins to eject.

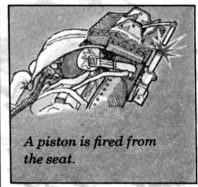

A piston is fired from the seat.

The piston draws out the parachute from its pack.

the canopy flies off the cockpit.

The seat falls away as the main parachute billows open.

The fully opened parachute now supports the pilot as he glides slowly to earth.

Electronic Eyes

Many inventions are made during wartime, because the need to make new weapons and defences becomes very urgent. Some inventions find other uses after the war is over. Radar is such an invention. It was first used to detect enemy aircraft and ships, but nowadays it helps ships and aircraft to travel safely. It also helps to find out what the weather will be; it makes discoveries about the planets, and helps to trap speeding motorists!

Radar was invented during World War II, and the name stands for radio detection and ranging. We see objects because light rays are reflected from them to our eyes. Radar is a way of doing the same thing with **radio waves**. A radar **transmitter** sends out **radio signals**, and objects in their path reflect the signals back to the transmitter. The transmitter picks up the reflected signals and shows them on a screen like a television screen.

Above: *A radar aerial, which can be seen (below), is fixed high on the boat's mast, so that it is able to 'see' a long way off.*

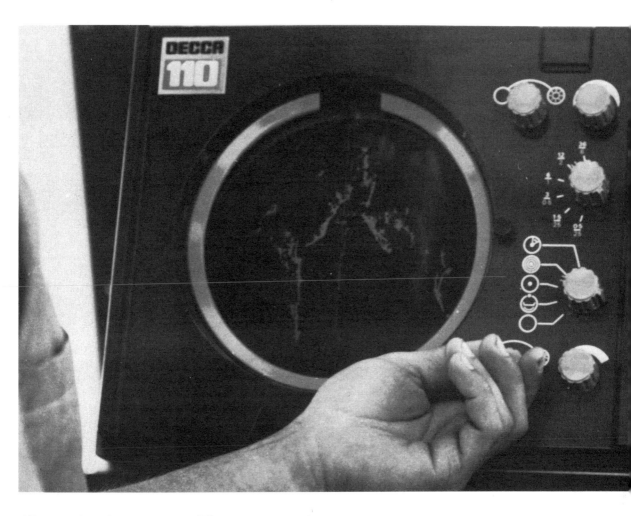

Above: *A radar screen.*
Below: *Ship (A) sends out radar signals in all directions and receives the signals reflected back from ship (B).*

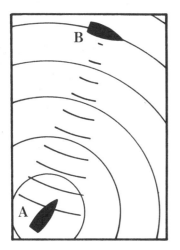

The time it takes for the signals to return to the transmitter depends on the distance of the objects. The screen shows the objects around the transmitter at their various distances.

A ship with radar equipment is able to see all the ships around it at a single glance at the screen. This makes it easier to **navigate**. Furthermore, radar signals travel through fog and the dark so the ship can continue to travel safely at all times. Radar also has a greater range than the eye, and aircraft many kilometres away can be detected by radar. Airports make use of radar to keep track of aircraft and make sure that they all keep to separate flight paths (you can read about airports on pages 140 and 141).

Aircraft and **meteorologists** can get some idea of the weather that lies ahead by using radar to detect **air turbulence** and storms. **Astronomers** bounce radar signals off planets to work out their distances and rates of spin. While police can use radar to measure the speed at which cars are travelling.

Instant Answers

People have looked for help with **arithmetic** ever since they began to use numbers. There have been the **abacus, logarithms** and the **slide rule,** but all these require some knowledge of mathematics to use. An adding machine was invented more than 300 years ago. It worked like the cash register in every shop works. Such machines need no learning, but they are difficult to use.

Now we have a machine that will give an instant and correct answer to the most difficult arithmetic sum—the pocket electronic calculator. The numbers are simply fed into the calculator by pressing buttons, and the answer flashes up on the **display panel** far faster than you can think.

The 'brain' of the calculator is called an integrated circuit. It is a minute chip of **silicon** containing thousands of tiny **transistors** and other electronic parts.

Right: *The inside of a pocket calculator.* **Left:** *An integrated circuit, the brain of a calculator, compared in size to a postage stamp.*

The integrated circuit was first developed for the American space programme. Ordinary transistors and circuitry are too heavy and bulky to fit into a small, light spacecraft. A whole new science had to be developed to produce these 'brains'. They work by changing every number into binary code, so that the number becomes an electric current switching on and off. One is on, two is on-off, three is on-on, four is on-off-off, five is on-off-on, and so on. The numbers become groups of electric pulses, and the brain of the calculator simply repeatedly adds or takes away to do the sums. It can make millions of separate additions or subtractions in a second, so that even the most difficult sum takes hardly any time at all.

However, the calculator will never replace the human brain for simple sums. Although it can work out an answer in less than a second, the whole calculation is much more lengthy because it takes some time to use the calculator. If you had to use a calculator every time you needed to count some money when shopping, you would be wasting time for a lot of people.

Buttons

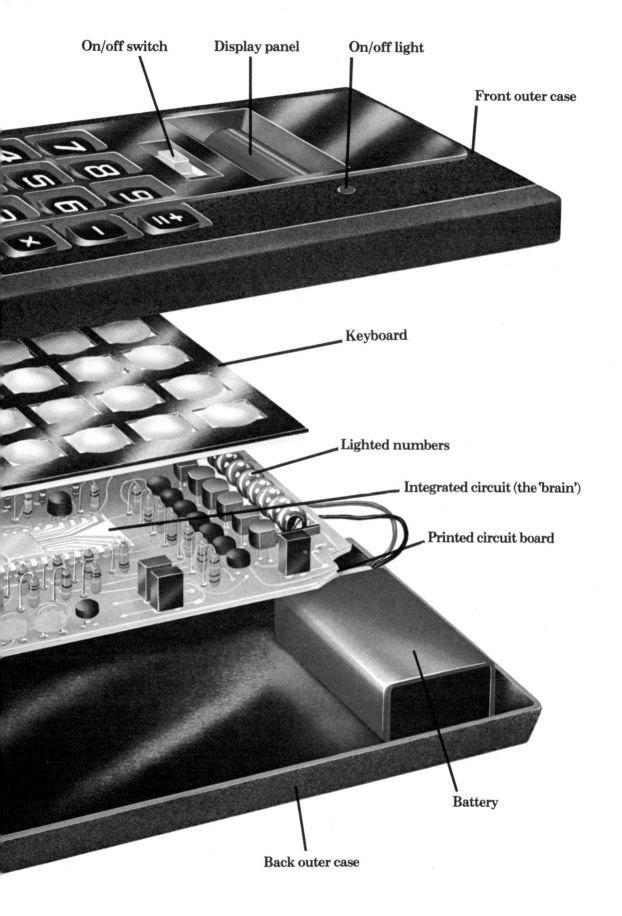

On/off switch   Display panel   On/off light

Front outer case

Keyboard

Lighted numbers

Integrated circuit (the 'brain')

Printed circuit board

Battery

Back outer case

195

A Meal in Seconds

The very latest oven can cook food in a few moments, yet it does not contain a roaring flame nor any red-hot cooking **elements**. This kind of oven is called a micro-wave oven. Microwaves are invisible rays. They are like infra-red rays, the invisible heat rays that reach us from the Sun or an electric fire, and also like radio waves, which can go through walls. Microwaves can also go through food. They therefore heat the inside of an object as well as the outside.

In a microwave oven, the food is cooked by bathing it in a beam of microwaves. Because the inside of the food

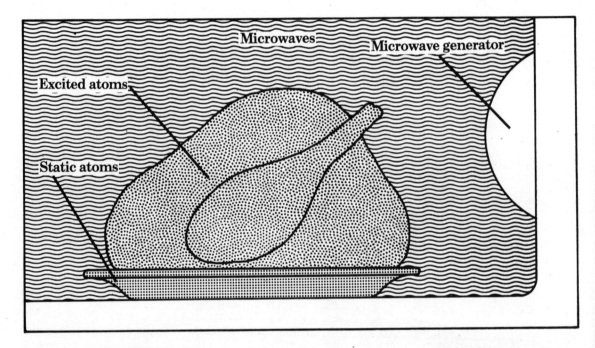

is heated as quickly as the outside, it does not need to cook for a long time. In a normal oven, the outside heats up very quickly, but it takes a long time for the heat to get to the centre. If we try to cook a piece of meat quickly by placing it in a very hot oven, the outside will soon be cooked but the inside will still be raw. In a microwave oven, the whole piece of meat is cooked right through in a few minutes.

Microwave ovens are not only used to cook meals quickly from raw food. In many canteens and snack bars, they are used to heat up food that has already been cooked. This precooked food is packed and then frozen to keep it fresh. The microwave oven then heats the food right through so that the food can be ready to eat in a few seconds. This saves time in places where large numbers

Above: *Microwaves go right through food and cook it from the inside outwards. In an ordinary cooker or oven, it takes a long time for the heat to get to the centre of the food to cook it completely.*

196

of people require food quickly. Airline staff give meals to their passengers prepared in this way. Reheating also saves space as well as time.

Microwave ovens mean people can buy hot meals from automatic **vending** machines. When a coin is put in the machine the food comes out in a frozen package. The buyer then simply puts it in a microwave oven placed by the vending machine to heat it.

The microwave oven operates on a similar principle to radar. Both devices work by bombarding an object by micro-wave patterns. In the case of the oven, to cook something and with radar to 'see' something by its microwave echo.

Below: *A steak will take only a few minutes to cook in this modern microwave oven. All you have to do is select the right time for the food you have put in the oven, press the start button, and when your food is cooked a light will come on to tell you it's ready.*

Automation

The people of many countries nowadays can lead comfortable lives because so many machines work for them. Labour-saving machines make housework easier in the home, but more important are the automatic machines that make things in factories. By automation, which means the use of machines in every stage of making goods, people can have more time to spend away from work and take the chance to do what they want with their free time.

Automation also means that many new kinds of goods can be made that could not possibly be made by

Opposite page: *The automatic machines in which chocolate drops are coated with sugar.* **Left:** *A view of the cold, metal rollers (top and bottom of diagram) showing how the liquid chocolate is squeezed into hard drops.*

hand, such as the tiny **circuits** used in calculators (you can read about calculators on pages 194 and 195). The photograph and drawing show how small sugar-coated chocolate sweets are made by machines. Although the sweets could be made by hand, it would take a long time to do so. The machine-made sweets are just as good as hand-made ones and are much cheaper.

First the liquid chocolate flows between two cold metal rollers studded with holes. The chocolate passes through the rollers and, because the metal rollers are so cold, the chocolate-drops set immediately in the holes and then fall out into a **conveyor.** Then the drops are all tumbled together in a **revolving** drum to make them smooth. The smooth drops then go to another revolving drum where a sugary liquid is added. As they fall through the liquid, each drop becomes coated with sugar. The drops are then dried by warm air blowing over them. More coatings of sugar are added in the same way to give a hard covering of sugar.

Finally, a coloured sugar coating is added and the sweets are polished before being packed. Sweets of different colours are made separately and then they are all mixed together before packing.

A Million Times Larger

A vast amount of knowledge lies hidden from our eyes because it is either too far away from us, or too small for us to see. But we have ways that can make the power of our eyes much greater. The most powerful **telescopes** can allow us to see out to the edges of the Universe, and the most powerful **microscopes** can peer into the tiny molecules of which everything is made.

An ordinary microscope can **magnify** anything up to 2,000 times larger than we can see it. Even this is not large enough to see the very smallest parts of things. An electron microscope uses beams of **electrons** instead of light. Electrons are very small particles, even smaller than atoms. The electron microscope has **magnets**

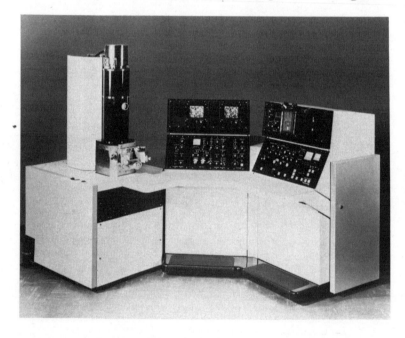

instead of **lenses**. These magnets bend electron beams and make **images** we can see, just as lenses bend light rays to make images we can see.

The **specimen** to be examined is placed inside the electron microscope and a magnified image consisting of electrons is made. We cannot see such an image because electrons are invisible. The electron beam is fed into what looks like a television screen which is part of the electron microscope, and the image of the specimen shows on the screen. With the electron microscope we can see things magnified more than a million times. This is great enough to see groups of atoms.

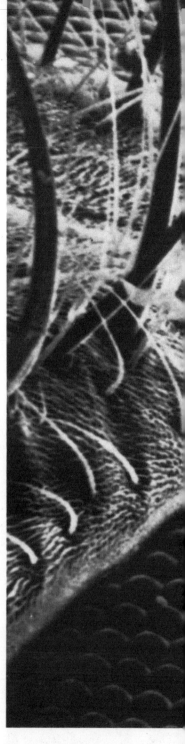

Above left: *An electron microscope. The high-magnification pictures that the electron microscope produces are of great value to modern science.*

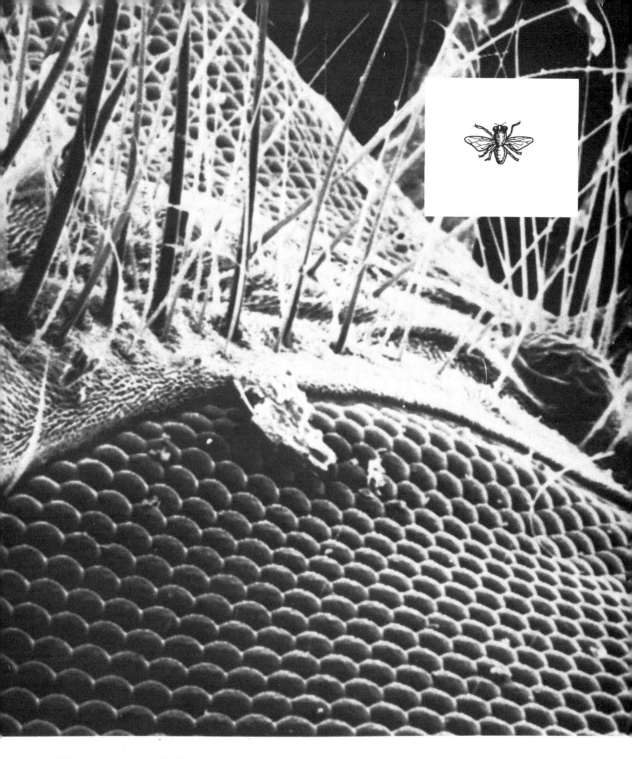

With a new kind of microscope using lasers (you can read about lasers on pages 22 and 23), magnifications of hundreds of millions can be obtained. It is so powerful that for the first time we can look inside the atom.

The theory behind the electron microscope was first put forward as early this century as 1924. And in 1933 the first 'supermicroscope' was built. This microscope could magnify an object up to about 12,000 times its original size.

Above: *a view of the eye of a fly taken with an electron microscope. It is magnified 250 times.*
Inset: *A drawing of a fly, actual size.*

Seeing Around Corners

You may have often thought how useful it would be if you were able to see around corners and not be seen by anyone. Doctors have always wanted to be able to see inside people without having to cut them open. Now both these dreams have come true through the invention of what is called fibre optics.

Fibre optics works because of total internal reflection. This means that at certain angles to a surface, light is reflected instead of passing through the surface. In fibre optics, a thin fibre of glass or plastic keeps in the light. The light goes in one end of the fibre and travels along it instead of going through it, because the light is reflected whenever it hits the inside of the fibre. It cannot escape and so passes along the fibre and comes out at the other end, just as bright as it went in.

In fibre optics, a rod made up of a bundle of these very thin fibres is used. Using a **lens**, a picture goes into one end of the rod. The light travels along the fibres so that the picture can be seen at the other end. The rod can

Right: *Light directed down a glass fibre is reflected from side to side. It is only seen when it comes out at the other end of the fibre.* **Opposite page:** *Fibre optics as an ornament.*

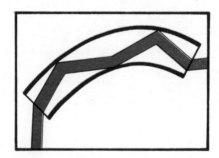

be bent into curves, tied in knots and the light will still stay inside the rod. So this kind of rod can be used to see round corners.

Doctors use fibre optics to look inside the body. A tiny camera is joined to a fibre optic rod and together they are passed into the body. The camera takes a picture inside the body and the picture travels back along the rod and out of the body. In this way, doctors can look inside the body without operating (you can read about this on pages 170 and 171).

If the fibres in the rod are twisted, the picture will be mixed into a pattern of dots which mean nothing. However, if this mixed picture is then put into an identical twisted rod, a clear picture will come out. In this way, fibre optics can be used to code pictures and messages. Only the correct fibre-optic rod will be able to obtain the correct picture or message.

Controlling the Weather

Below: A weather control aircraft seeds a cloud with 'dry ice', which is carbon dioxide frozen into crystals. These crystals are used to help make the clouds produce rain.

Weather control is one kind of power over nature that everyone would like to have. Making rain or sunshine when we need them would mean farmers could always have a good **harvest**. Clearing fog would save lives by reducing accidents on the road and would stop the long delays to aircraft at airports. Controlling vast storm clouds and hurricane winds would prevent flooding and loss of life. Strangely enough, even though our **civilization** has taken great steps forward with many discoveries, we have not learned how to control our weather completely. However, there are certain parts of our weather that we have learned to control.

Rain and snow fall from clouds because **water vapour** in the cloud collects on tiny particles of ice or dust and makes them grow into raindrops or snowflakes. Rain or snow can be made to fall from the cloud before it would do so naturally. This is done by seeding clouds. Seeding clouds means dropping **crystals** of dry ice (solid carbon dioxide) or salt from an aircraft.

In this way, rain can be made to fall on a dry area beneath the cloud or stop rain falling on a wet region which does not need the rain. Seeding may also clear fog, make a storm cloud lose its power, and stop hail stones building up to such a size that they damage **crops**. Seeding does not always work, but as it is used more and more, it will become more reliable.

Below left: *The cloud begins to change into a rain cloud after the crystals have been dropped.*
Below right: *Eventually, the cloud develops the shape of a typical storm cloud and rain begins to fall on the dry ground below.*

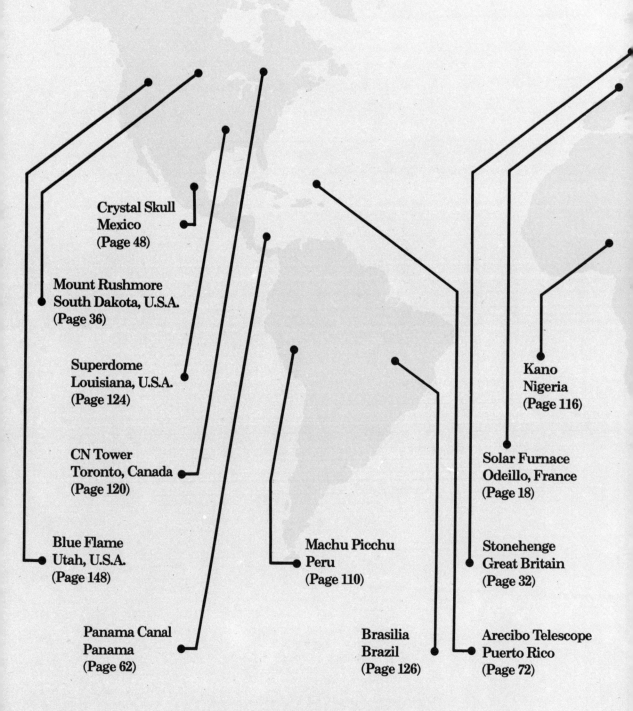

Crystal Skull
Mexico
(Page 48)

Mount Rushmore
South Dakota, U.S.A.
(Page 36)

Superdome
Louisiana, U.S.A.
(Page 124)

CN Tower
Toronto, Canada
(Page 120)

Blue Flame
Utah, U.S.A.
(Page 148)

Panama Canal
Panama
(Page 62)

Machu Picchu
Peru
(Page 110)

Kano
Nigeria
(Page 116)

Solar Furnace
Odeillo, France
(Page 18)

Stonehenge
Great Britain
(Page 32)

Brasilia
Brazil
(Page 126)

Arecibo Telescope
Puerto Rico
(Page 72)

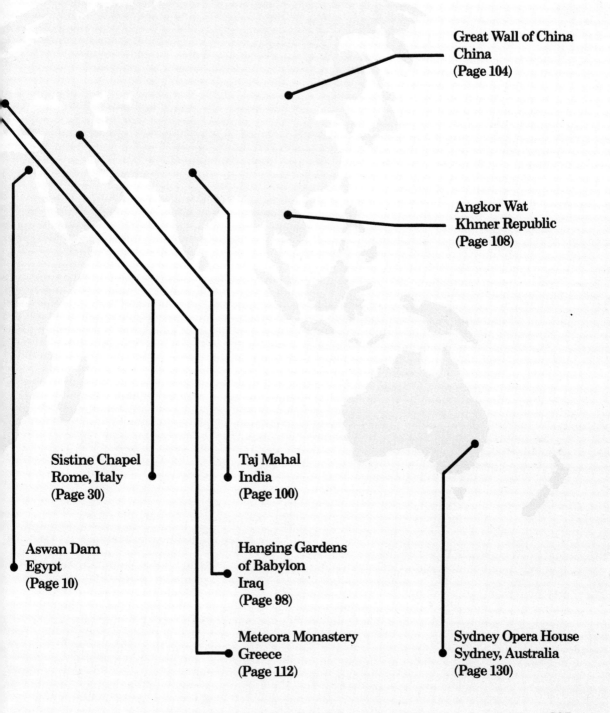

Great Wall of China
China
(Page 104)

Angkor Wat
Khmer Republic
(Page 108)

Sistine Chapel
Rome, Italy
(Page 30)

Taj Mahal
India
(Page 100)

Aswan Dam
Egypt
(Page 10)

Hanging Gardens
of Babylon
Iraq
(Page 98)

Meteora Monastery
Greece
(Page 112)

Sydney Opera House
Sydney, Australia
(Page 130)

Illustrated Glossary

A

Abacus The abacus has a set of wires threaded with beads. It is used to add up and subtract numbers. The beads on the wires stand for ones, tens, or hundreds, and calculations are made by moving the beads to and fro. The abacus was invented in ancient times and is still used in the East *(below)*.

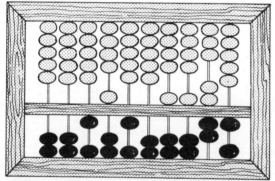

Adhesive An adhesive is a substance that sticks things together. Adhesives include glues made from animal remains, gums that come from plants, and resins made from chemicals.

Ailment Ailment is another word for illness.

Air turbulence Sometimes, aircraft meet movements of the air that produce a bumpy flight. The air is turbulent, meaning that it does not move smoothly. Air turbulence is not dangerous, because all aircraft are strong enough to withstand the bumps.

Alkali An alkali is a chemical substance that makes an acid (*see* Chemical) harmless. Strong alkalis can dissolve materials, and caustic soda (a very strong alkali) is used to remove paint from surfaces. We usually get stomach-ache because the liquid in our stomachs is too acid. We take a weak alkali, such as magnesia, to remove the extra acid.

Amateur An amateur is a person who does a job or performs a service without requiring monetary payment.

American football In American football, the players may carry the ball and can use their hands to block other players. There are eleven players in each team, and each tries to get the egg-shaped ball across their opponents' goal line *(below)*.

Anaesthetic An anaesthetic is a drug that stops pain. A *general* anaesthetic is given to put a patient to sleep during an operation so that he or she feels nothing at all. A *local* anaesthetic stops the pain from just one part of the body while the patient stays awake.

Anniversary An anniversary is the same day of each year that an important event happened. For example, your birthday is the anniversary of the day you were born.

Aperture An aperture is generally an opening of any kind.

Arabian Nights *The Arabian Nights* is a collection of stories that was first written in Arabic several centuries ago. It includes such famous tales as *Aladdin* and *Sinbad the Sailor*. The collection is also known as *A Thousand and One Nights*, because the stories are told by Scheherazade, a princess, who pleases a cruel sultan by telling him the stories for a thousand and one nights.

Archaeologist An archaeologist is a person who discovers things about the past from studying old buildings and remains. He may dig up the ruins and remains himself.

Architect An architect is a person who designs a new building.

Arena An arena is a large space or stage in which various sports or entertainments are performed.

Arithmetic We learn arithmetic so that we can use numbers. In arithmetic, we find out how to count and then how to add, subtract, multiply and divide numbers.

Astronaut Any person who travels in space is called an astronaut. Russian spacemen are also known as cosmonauts *(below)*.

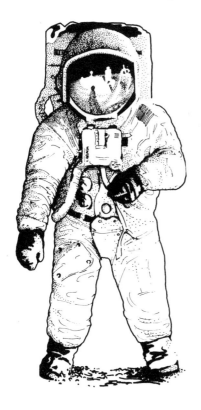

Astronomer An astronomer is a person who studies the bodies in the heavens, such as the Moon, Sun, planets, stars and galaxies (groups of stars far away in space).

Atmosphere Most of the planets that go around the Sun have an atmosphere, a layer of gases, above their surfaces. On Earth, the atmosphere is made of air.

Atom Everything is made up of very small particles called atoms. They are much too small to be seen, except in the most powerful microscopes.

Automatic machinery Any machine that can run itself without anyone needing to control it is automatic. For example, a refrigerator switches itself on and off automatically in order to keep things cold inside.

B

Bacteria Bacteria are also known as germs. They are very small living things and can only be seen with a microscope.

Bale A bale is a large bundle of a material such as hay and straw. The material is pressed together and bound up to make a bale.

Beacon A beacon is a device that makes a signal of some kind. Beacons were once bonfires that were lit on hills to warn people of invasion. Lighthouses have beacons of light to warn ships away from rocks. Radio beacons at airports guide aircraft by radio to land safely.

Borehole A borehole is a narrow hole that is drilled down through the rock to reach a deposit of oil or gas far underground.

Buoyancy Anything that floats has buoyancy; if it loses its buoyancy, it sinks. Things float in water if they are lighter than water.

Burnished gold A metal is burnished by rubbing or polishing to make it shiny.

Bypass A bypass is a road that leads around a town or city so that travellers do not have to cross through the town or city to reach somewhere else.

C

Calculation A calculation is made to solve a problem. Adding and subtracting numbers are simple calculations.

Calculator A calculator is a machine that performs calculations. Electronic calculators and computers can solve difficult problems very quickly indeed. A slide rule is a simple and cheap calculator (*see* Slide rule).

Canal A canal is a long waterway built to carry goods on boats and barges from one place to another. Canals are also dug to take water to various places where it is needed.

Capital The main city of a country, or of a county or province of a country, is called its capital. For example, London is the capital of Britain and Paris is the capital of France. Usually, the leaders of a country live in the capital.

Carbon Carbon is a substance that is found in several forms. Soot, coal and charcoal are black forms of carbon. Graphite, which is soft and slippery, and diamonds, which are hard and clear, are other forms of carbon (*below*).

Cargo The goods that a ship carries make up its cargo. A tanker carries a cargo of oil, for example.

Ceramic Ceramics are things that are made of baked clay. Pots, china cups and saucers, and tiles are all examples of ceramics.

Chasm A chasm is a deep and narrow crack in the ground.

Chemical A chemical is a pure substance that is not mixed with other substances. Salt is a chemical and so too is water.

Chute A chute is a sloping passage down which anything can travel, depending on how large the chute is.

Circuit A circuit is a path that comes back to its starting point. Cars go round and round a racing circuit, for example. In an electric circuit, an electric current flows from a power source around the circuit and back to the power source. On the way it flows through electrical devices and makes them work.

Civilization A civilization is a group of people who live together and make advances of certain kinds. They develop ways of writing and methods of government and make discoveries in the arts and sciences.

Cobra A cobra is a kind of snake. It is large and poisonous (*below*).

Cockpit The cockpit is the part of an aircraft used by the pilot and other members of the flying crew.

Collision A collision happens when any moving objects or vehicles crash or bump into each other.

Combustion Combustion is another word for burning. In an internal combustion engine, the fuel is burned inside the engine to provide power. Cars, aircraft and rockets have internal combustion engines.

Communications centre A communications centre is a place where messages all come together and then they are directed from one place to another.

Composer A composer is a person who creates music.

Computer systems A computer system is a group of electronic machines that can perform calculations very quickly (*see* Calculation; Electronics). For example, computer systems work out the amounts of money that people have in a bank.

Conquistadores The conquistadores were the Spanish adventurers who conquered the people of Mexico, Peru, and other parts of Central and South America in the 1500s.

Continent The continents are the great land areas of the world. They are Europe, Asia, Africa, Australia, North America, South America and Antarctica.

Convention A convention is a meeting of the members of a particular group of people.

Conveyor A conveyor carries substances, such as grain, from one machine to another.

Conveyor belt A conveyor belt is a moving belt used to carry things *(below)*.

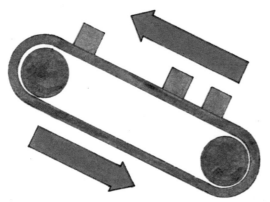

Crew A crew consists of all the people who work on a vehicle of any kind. It includes the captain of a ship and pilot of an airliner, as well as the engineers and the cabin staff who look after the passengers.

Crop A crop is any plant that is raised for use by people. Crops may be grown for eating, but also for making oils, fibres and other useful things *(below)*.

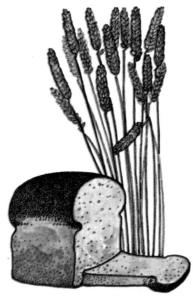

Crystal A crystal is a substance that is always found in pieces of similar shapes. Salt comes in crystals that are shaped like tiny cubes. Often the crystals stick together or have corners missing, so that the basic shape cannot easily be seen *(below)*.

Current The current of a river is the flow of water in it. An electric current is a flow of electricity through a length of wire or a piece of metal.

Curvature The curvature of an object is the amount by which it curves. The curvature of the Earth is so slight that it cannot normally be seen. However, it becomes obvious as you sail away from the shore and the coastline disappears over the horizon.

211

D

Declaration of Independence The Declaration of Independence declared that the colonies which British people had founded in North America were free and no longer governed by Great Britain. It was signed in 1776 and marks the founding of the United States of America.

Design A design is a plan or outline of something that is to be made. It is also the appearance of a pattern or a shape.

Device A device is a machine or invention of any kind that performs a useful purpose. For example, a kettle is a device used for boiling water.

Dies Wire is made by forcing metal rods through small holes in blocks to squeeze the metal and form wire. The blocks with the holes are called dies *(below)*.

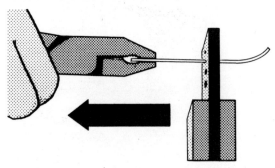

Display panel A panel containing instruments that give information is called a display panel. The indicator board at a railway station, the speedometer and other instruments in a car, and the numbers that light up in a pocket calculator are all examples of display panels.

Dome A dome is a roof shaped like one half of a sphere or ball *(below)*.

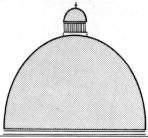

Dyke A dyke is a wall or bank built to stop the sea or a river from flooding the land.

E

Electric generator An electric generator is a machine that makes electricity. In it, a coil of wire spins in relation to a magnetic field, and an electric current is produced in the coil (*see* Magnetic field).

Electric signal Devices such as the mouthpiece of a telephone and the pick-up in a gramophone produce an electric signal. The signal varies in the same way as the sound spoken into the telephone or on the gramophone record varies. The signal therefore carries the characteristics of the sound, and enables the sound to be taken or transmitted from one place to another.

Electron An electron is a very tiny particle of electricity. Atoms contain several electrons (*see* Atoms).

Electronic circuit or electric circuit Every electrical machine contains wires through which electricity flows to make the machine work. The path that the electricity follows is called an electric or electronic circuit.

Electronics Electronics is a branch of science that deals with electrical machines that work by controlling the flow of electrons through a circuit (*see* Electron; Electronic circuit). These machines include television, radio, the gramophone and tape recorder.

Element Everything in the universe is made up either of pure elements or of compounds in which elements are combined together. Oxygen and nitrogen are elements, so that air is a mixture of elements. Water is a compound of oxygen with hydrogen, another element. Just over a hundred elements are known, but many of these are rare. Common elements include iron, aluminium, gold, silver, copper, iodine and carbon (*see* Carbon).

Elevate Elevate means to raise in height or to lift.

Emergency An emergency happens when something has to be done very quickly, usually without warning. When someone has an accident, getting a doctor is an emergency.

Engineer An engineer is a person who works in engineering.

Engineering Engineering is the branch of science in which knowledge is put to use. It includes making machines of all kinds in order to build roads and bridges, ships, aeroplanes, railways and reservoirs and power stations.

Estuary An estuary is the part of a river near its mouth where it widens and comes to the sea *(below)*.

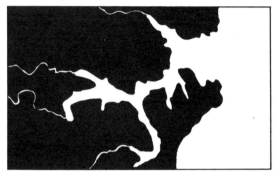

Excavate Excavate means to dig up or dig out, usually earth or stone.

Exhibition An exhibition is a special collection of objects that people come to see. The objects could be a group of paintings by one artist, or all the new motor cars of a particular year, for example.

Expedition An expedition is a special journey, often made to explore an unknown region.

F

Fabric Fabric is a word for cloth *(below)*.

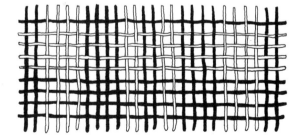

Factory A factory is a building or group of buildings in which something is made.

Fertile land Land on which crops grow well is called fertile *(see Crop)*.

Fibre A fibre is a very thin thread.

Fission Fission occurs when anything breaks apart. In nuclear fission, atoms break apart *(see Atom)*.

Flexible Anything is flexible if it bends without breaking.

Fortress A building that is built to be strong enough to withstand enemy attacks is a fortress.

Foundations The foundations of a building are the bottom part of the building that enters the ground. They are strong enough to support the building.

Framework A framework is a group of beams or girders connected together to make a support for a building or any other kind of structure *(below)*.

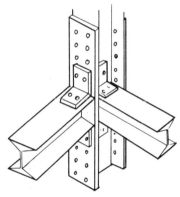

Friction When anything that moves is left to move on a level surface without pushing it or powering it in any way, it will come to a stop. For example, a ball sent rolling across a lawn comes to a stop. Friction is the force that makes it slow down and stop. It happens because of the resistance of the surface.

Furnace A furnace is a box or chamber in which things are heated to a great heat.

G

Glide path As an aircraft comes in to land at an airport, it follows a set course that brings it safely down to the runway. This course is called a glide path.

Gorge A gorge is a deep, narrow valley with steep, rocky sides.

H

Harvest A harvest takes place when crops become ripe and are gathered in.

Hindu religion The Hindu religion is the main religion of India. It is also followed in other Eastern countries. Hindus believe that their souls live on after death and move to another body.

Horizontal Anything that is flat and level, such as the surface of a table, is horizontal.

Hull The hull is the main body of a boat or any other floating craft *(below)*.

Hydraulic A hydraulic machine is operated by a liquid inside it. When a car driver operates the brakes of a car, he or she steps on a pedal which causes an increase in the pressure of liquid inside a pipe connected to the brakes. The increase in pressure makes the brakes work.

I

Ice yacht An ice yacht is just like an ordinary yacht except that it sails over ice on runners instead of floating in water.

Image An image of anything is a view of it formed by a mirror or a lens *(see* Lens*)*.

Independence Any country that governs itself is an independent country. Some countries are colonies; that is, they are governed by other countries. When a colony begins to govern itself, it gains independence.

K

Keyboard The keyboard is the set of keys that the fingers touch when playing an instrument like the piano or organ *(below)*.

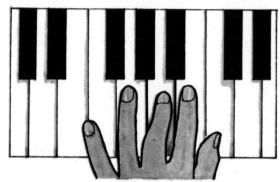

Kiln A kiln is a furnace used to make pottery. Pots are made by shaping wet, soft clay and then baking them in kilns to harden them.

L

Legend A legend is an ancient story that people still tell.

Lens A magnifying glass is a lens, and the round pieces of glass in spectacles are lenses. Lenses form images *(see* Image*)*. They are used in cameras, telescopes and microscopes.

Linear induction motor The linear induction motor is a kind of motor that works by magnetism. It can be used to move a vehicle along a track. The track has electromagnets (magnets powered by electricity) which produce a magnetic field that pulls the vehicle along *(see* Magnetic field*)*.

Logarithms Logarithms are tables that help to multiply or divide numbers. The logarithms of the numbers are other numbers that you look up in the tables. To multiply the first numbers, you add their logarithms together and then look up the answer in the tables.

Lottery A lottery is a kind of competition. Tickets are sold to get money for the prizes. The winners are chosen by taking the winning tickets out of a hat or by some other chance method.

Lunar module The lunar module is the part of the Apollo spacecraft that landed on the Moon.

M

Magnet A magnet is a piece of metal, usually iron or steel, that attracts another magnet. Electromagnets become magnets when an electric current flows through them *(below)*.

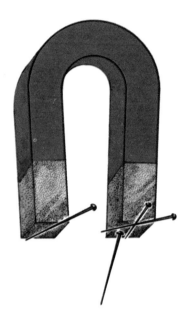

Magnetic Anything that acts like a magnet is magnetic.

Magnetic field A magnetic field surrounds every magnet. It is invisible. When the magnetic field of one magnet touches the magnetic field of another, the two magnets will be pulled towards each other or, in some cases, pushed apart.

Magnetic tape The tape in a tape recorder and several other machines is magnetic. It records an electric signal as a pattern of magnetism in the tape *(see* Electric signal).

Magnify An image of an object that is bigger than the object itself is magnified *(see* Image). A magnifying glass and a microscope magnify.

Meteorologist A person who studies the weather and forecasts the weather to come is called a meteorologist.

Microscope A microscope makes images of objects that are very much bigger than the object itself *(see* Image).

Minaret A minaret is a tower that is built as part of a mosque, the place of worship in the Moslem religion. The muezzin (priest) calls the people to prayer from the minaret.

Mission control During a spaceflight, the spacemen are in contact with the ground and all their orders come from mission control by radio.

Monastery A monastery is a place where monks live. Monks are men who give all their lives to serving a religion.

Mongol A Mongol is a person who lives in Mongolia, a country to the north of China. In the 1200s, the Mongols gained a huge empire that covered most of Asia.

Morse signal Morse is a code made up of short and long signals (dots and dashes). Each group of dots and dashes stands for a letter or number. The signals are sent by radio or by flashing lights *(below)*.

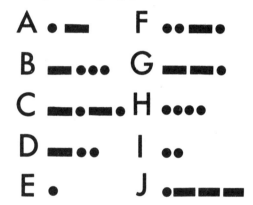

N

Navigate The navigator of a ship or aircraft works out the direction that the ship or aircraft must take to get to the place where it is going.

Nutrients Nutrients are substances that help to support life. Food is made up of nutrients.

O

Observatory Astronomers work in an observatory. They use telescopes to study the planets and stars in the heavens.

Orchestra An orchestra is a large group of musicians.

P

Patent An invention is patented or gets a patent to stop other people from selling the invention without the inventor's permission.

Patient A patient is anyone who is treated by a doctor.

Pedestal A pedestal is a support. The tall block of stone on which a statue stands is called a pedestal.

Performer Anyone who sings, dances, plays an instrument or generally entertains people is called a performer.

Pilgrim A pilgrim is a person who makes a special journey to a holy town or place as part of his religion.

Pinnacle Pinnacles are slender, pointed formations on the tops of buildings such as churches, and on mountains *(below)*.

Piston engine A piston engine is one in which the fuel burns to make a piston (a disc at the end of a rod) move up and down. Most cars have a piston engine. The up-and-down motion is changed into circular motion to power the wheels.

Pithead The pithead of a coal mine is the group of buildings at the surface. From the pithead, the miners enter the mine by going down in lifts.

Plague A disease that spreads and kills people and animals.

Plinth A plinth is a block on which an object stands or is supported.

Polder A polder is an area of low land that was once under water but has since been drained.

Pollution Air or water that contains anything that may harm people, animals or crops is polluted. The pollution it contains usually comes from factories (*see* Factory).

Portable Anything that is small and light enough to be carried with ease by one person is portable.

Prestressed concrete A block of concrete is very strong when it is being squeezed, but not if it is being pulled apart. In building, concrete blocks are squeezed by laying rods or cables in them and then tightening the rods or cables. This kind of concrete is called prestressed concrete.

Printing plate In printing, ink is applied to a printing plate containing an impression of the words and pictures on a page. The inked plate is then pressed on sheets of paper to print the page *(below)*.

Propeller A propeller is a set of blades like a fan that spins to drive an aircraft or boat through the air or water.

Protein Food contains three main kinds of substances that help to support life. Protein is one of them, and it helps to build the body.

Pulley A pulley is made up of a rope passing over a wheel or group of wheels. A heavy object is attached to one end of the rope and the other end is pulled. The pulley wheels make it easier to lift the object.

Q

Quarry A quarry is a large hole that is dug in the ground to get stone for building.

R

Radio signal Radio signals are sent from the radio station to your home. The signals are changed into sound or a picture in a radio or television set.

Radio wave A radio wave flows from the transmitter of a radio or television station to the aerial connected to the radio or television set in your home. The wave carries the radio signals that produce the sound or the picture.

Ravine A ravine is a narrow and very deep valley.

Rebel A rebel is a person who does not agree with the people in charge of him or who govern him. Rebels try to overcome those who lead or control them and then govern themselves.

Record A record is a way of storing knowledge or information. A gramophone record stores a piece of music so that it can be heard at any time.

Remedy A remedy is an action or treatment that makes someone or something better.

Replica A replica is an exact copy of something.

Reservoir A reservoir is a huge tank or a lake that stores drinking water.

Resident Anyone who lives in a particular place is a resident of that place. A residential section of a town or city contains people's homes.

Revolve Something that is revolving is either moving in a circle around something else or it is spinning around its own centre.

Revolving drum A revolving drum is a spinning container.

Rotate Something that is rotating is spinning around its own centre.

S

Sacrifice A sacrifice takes place when an animal or person is killed as part of a religion. However, Christianity and other major religions do not believe in sacrifice.

Satellite A satellite is a body that moves around, or orbits, another body in space. The Moon is a satellite of the Earth. Many man-made satellites orbit the Earth.

Scientific observation Scientists gain knowledge by looking at things or making observations to see how they work.

Scientific research Scientists do research when they try to discover new things. They think up and do experiments that they hope will show something new.

Scientist A scientist makes a study of science. In science, knowledge is gained by observation and research (*see* Scientific observation; Scientific research). All knowledge in science has to be tested and shown to be true.

Scribe In ancient times, before many people could write, a scribe used to write things down for people.

Sculptor A sculptor is a person who makes statues or carves shapes.

Scythe A scythe is a sharp blade with a long handle that is used to cut long grass or ripe corn and other cereal crops.

Self-propelled vehicle A vehicle that is self-propelled can run under its own power and does not need to be pedalled or pushed. A motor car and an aeroplane are self-propelled but a bicycle is not.

Semiconductor A semiconductor is a substance that is used in electronics because the flow of electrons through it can easily be controlled. Transistors are made of semiconductors (*see* Electronics; Transistor).

Shackle Shackles are metal bands fastened around the wrists or ankles to make someone a prisoner (*below*).

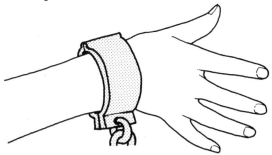

Shaft A shaft is either a deep or long hole or passage made in the ground or in a building, or it is a long rod.

Shoal A large group of fish is called a shoal.

Sickle A sickle is a curved blade with a short handle used for cutting grass and weeds (*below*).

Signal A signal is a sign to show that an action may take place. An electric signal is a flow of electric current that is changed into something else. In a radio set, signals are changed into sound, and in a television set, into a picture.

Silicon Silicon is an element that is used as a semiconductor (*see* Element; Semiconductor).

Site A place where an important event such as a battle once happened is the site of that event. In archaeology, a site is a place where ancient ruins or remains are found (*see* Archaeologist).

Slide rule A slide rule is used to make calculations (*see* Calculation). It has two rulers marked with numbers, and one slides inside the other. By moving the rulers to and fro, numbers can be easily multiplied and divided.

Soil erosion Land may lose its soil by the action of wind and rain. When this happens, soil erosion takes place.

Solar cell A solar cell turns sunlight into electricity.

Solar furnace A solar furnace collects the hot rays in sunlight and, by focusing them, uses them to heat things.

Solar panel A solar panel is a panel containing solar cells, or a panel that collects the Sun's heat.

Sound barrier The speed of sound is about a thousand kilometres an hour at high altitudes in the sky. Special aircraft are needed to fly faster than sound, and as they reach the speed of sound, they are said to pass through the sound barrier. In fact, no actual barrier exists, but a bang is heard when an aircraft flies faster than sound. The bang is caused by the action of sound waves at these speeds and not by an explosion.

Span The span of a bridge is the distance between the ends or supports (*below*).

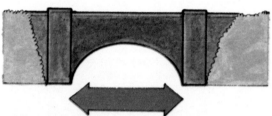

Specimen In a microscope, the specimen is the object or part of the object that is being examined.

Spiral A spiral is a line that curves in on itself. The groove on a gramophone record follows a spiral path. The coils of a long spring are often said to be in a spiral, but they are in fact in a helix.

Stadium A stadium is a huge building mainly used for sports. It has a large track or pitch surrounded by seats and stands for the spectators.

Structure A structure is anything that is made by putting several separate parts together. A building is often referred to as a structure.

Studio A studio is a large room where radio or television programmes, sound recordings or cinema films are made. Lessons in dancing are also held in a studio, and a painter or sculptor works in a studio.

Suburb The suburbs of a city are the districts that are located outside the centre of the city.

Supersonic airliner A supersonic airliner is an airliner that can fly faster than sound (*see* Sound barrier).

Symbol A symbol is an object or a picture of an object that stands for something else. For example, a picture of a dove is often used as a symbol of peace *(below)*.

System A system is a particular way of doing something in which rules are followed every time. A system is also a particular group of things, such as a road system.

T

Talent Anyone who has a talent or is talented is very good at doing something.

Telescope A telescope is an instrument that makes distant objects seem nearer than they are.

Transistor A transistor is an electronic device that increases the power of an electric signal passing through it. It is made of a semiconductor such as silicon (*see* Electronics; Semiconductor; Signal; Silicon).

Transmit To transmit something means to send it to someone over a distance.

Transmitter A transmitter sends out radio waves that carry electric signals (*see* Radio signal; Radio wave).

Tread A tank or tractor runs on a belt made up of separate pieces of metal called treads.

Tripod A tripod is a support that has three legs. A camera is placed on a tripod to make it steady.

Turbine A turbine is a set of blades like a fan. It turns as liquids or gases flow through the blades. A windmill is a kind of air turbine.

V

Vegetation The vegetation of a region consists of all the kinds of plants that grow in that area.

Vein A vein in rock is a line of mineral running through the rock. In the body, a vein carries blood to the heart.

Vend A person or machine that vends something is selling it.

Victim A victim is someone who is harmed in any way.

Video Video means to do with vision. A video recorder records a picture, and video signals are electric signals that can be changed into a picture.

Video display unit A video display unit produces information that can be seen, usually in the form of numbers that light up.

Villa A villa is a large country house.

Volcanic rock The molten lava that pours from volcanoes cools and hardens to produce volcanic rock.

W

Water vapour Water vapour is a form of water that is an invisible gas. Water always produces some water vapour in the air.

Windlass A windlass is a cylinder that is pushed round to wind up a rope *(below)*.

Y

Yarn Fibres of wool and other materials are spun together to make strands of yarn. The yarn is woven or knitted to make cloth.

INDEX

Where figures are in bold type this shows that they refer to illustrations or photographs.

10/11 Douglas Dickins. 12/13 Swiss National Tourist Office. 14/17 United Kingdom Atomic Energy Authority. 18/19 Gamma. 20/21 Sodel. 22/23 Ferranti Ltd, Paul Brierley. 24/25 Central Electricity Generating Board. 26/27 Shell International Petroleum Company. 28/29 National Coal Board. 30/31 Scala. 32/33 British Tourist Authority. 36/37 Picturepoint Ltd, Robert Harding Associates. 38/39 Outlook Films Ltd. 40/41 Camera Press Ltd. 42/43 Loren McIntyre. 44/45 Netherlands National Tourist Office. 46/47 Scala. 48/49 British Museum. 50/51 Picturepoint Limited. 52/53 Cement and Concrete Association. 54/55 Spectrum Colour Library, Aerofilms Ltd. 56/57 Pat Morris. 58/59 Douglas Dickins, Triborough Bridge and Tunnel Authority. 60/61 Popperfoto. 62/63 Robert Harding Associates. 64/65 Netherlands National Tourist Office. 66/67 Douglas Dickins. 68/69 Geographical Coloured Slides. 70/71 Spectrum Colour Library. 72/73 Arecibo Observatory, Cornell University. 76/77 Thames Television. 78/79 Polaroid Corporation. 80/81 Paul Brierley. 82/83 Theorem Publishing Ltd. 84/85 Walt Disney Productions Ltd, United Artists. 90/91 Mike Rock. 92/93 Outlook Films Ltd. 94/95 Douglas Dickins. 100/101 Ken Lowther. 102/103 Douglas Dickins. 104/105 J. Allan Cash. 106/107 H.J. Pike. 108/109 Douglas Dickins, Outlook Films Ltd. 110/111 Robert Harding Associates. 112/113 Douglas Dickins. 116/117 J. Allan Cash. 118/119 Transamerica Corporation. 120/121 Canadian National Railways. 124/125 Louisiana Superdome. 126/127 Robert Harding Associates. 128/129 Douglas Dickins. 130/131 Australian Information Service, Robert Harding Associates. 132/133 U.S. Navy. 134/135 British Airways. 140/141 Civil Aviation Authority. 144/145 British Rail Hovercraft Ltd, Novosti Press Agency. 146/147 Globtik Tankers Ltd. 148/149 Popperfoto. 152/153 Société de "l'Aerotrain". 154/155 Paul Brierley. 156/157 Ciba-Geigy (UK) Ltd. 160/161 Yardley of London Ltd. 162/163 Theorem Publishing Ltd, Paul Brierley. 168/169 Vickers Ltd. 172/173 British Acupuncture Association and Register. 176/177 St. Mary's Hospital Medical School. 182/183 John Prizeman. 184/185 Norwich Union Insurance Group, Pat Morris. 188/189 Robert Harding Associates, Popperfoto. 192/193 Decca Radar Ltd. 196/197 Paul Brierley. 198/199 Rowntree Mackintosh. 200/201 Cambridge Inst. 202/203 Etcetera.